George B. Simpson

The vital forces in nature, and the rights of man

George B. Simpson

The vital forces in nature, and the rights of man

ISBN/EAN: 9783337775483

Printed in Europe, USA, Canada, Australia, Japan

Cover: Foto ©ninafisch / pixelio.de

More available books at **www.hansebooks.com**

THE

VITAL FORCES IN NATURE

AND THE

RIGHTS OF MAN,

BY

GEORGE B. SIMPSON.

There is a divinity within the human soul that moves Man onward to
noble deeds; it inspires with hope, and bids him *live*.

WASHINGTON :
PRINTED BY R. A. WATERS.
1862.

TO THE PUBLIC.

—o—

In submitting these writings to the people, the author need not remind them that the subject is not continuously connected. They are the *outcroppings* of a great system, embracing science, philosophy, and divinity.

Without means, without friends, without books, the author set out upon the uncertain sea of research—of investigation, resolved to *learn* by practical observation that which was written in the great Book of Nature, whose God-imprinted pages were every where spread out before him.

From effects he reasoned to causes ; from causes he reasoned to prior causes, and thence onward still to prior causes, and thus onward through the great Arcana of Nature up to God.

He first discovered *within* himself a power, motive in its character, and *obedient* to his *will*. He then discovered that this motive power was the *servant* of his *will*, which *will* was also the immediate *agent* of himself—REASON. He next sought the *office* of Reason. In this he found his *interior Being*, the divinely instituted *Man*, not unlike an *Umpire*, ordering judgment on impressions impelled *through* the senses to the *sensorium* of the brain, where *He* sits, in state, and receives all ideas, thoughts and impressions, good and bad, analyzing and estimating each according to its intrinsic merit, upon which examination judgment is rendered and the decree passed over to *will* for execution. The positive now *acts* on the negative—the *greater mind*, which is located in the *Cerebrum*, now acts on the *lesser mind*, which is located in the *Cerebelum*, which action is simply an effort or *emotion* of the *will*, putting into *locomotion* all the parts of his physical system, thus performing the *acts* which his *reason* dictates.

Having now discovered the *vital forces* of his own BEING—the process of *learning*, and the *faculty* of choosing between good and comparative evil, he looked out upon the great Book— Nature's own. Here he saw impressed upon the surface of things the *type* of an internal *reality*; this reality was the *vital force* which impelled the development of the external *Form*; and in these external forms he discovered the concentrated *germ* of *reproduction*; thus onward *ad infinitum*.

He saw, again, not by his occult vision, but by his *Reason*, that the world of forms and substances with which he himself is connected and of which he constitutes a part, *is now in process of refining*, and that no form *can descend* below its own development, but that it must, by virtue of the *law* giving it vitality, *ascend* in the scale and order of creation.

Thus he found that all forms are in a *transition state;* that *old* forms are incessantly passing out of existence, while the world is as incessantly being re-peopled with *new* and living forms, *each refining and concentrating a part of itself for the purpose of reproducing its "Kind,"* and at the same time sustaining the higher organisms which, in their order, *have been unfolded through similar forms.*

Thus it will appear that the only substances, things, or Beings ever *created* were *forms;* and that all *old forms* are passing away, and *new forms* are constantly taking their place; hence it is, *that creation is as effectually going on to day as it was six thousand years ago, or even six hundred thousand years ago.*

Thus it will be seen that this subject embraces in its comprehensive scope all causes, all effects, and all subjects which can be contemplated by the human mind. And, in treating of the laws or developing forces alike *inherent* in each atom and each world, it is apparent that one atom cannot exist without the *pre-existence* of other atoms, and that one world cannot exist without the *pre-existence* of other worlds, and that each are alike the *tangible form* of an *interior force* which, on *analysis*, is found to revert from *effect to cause*, and from cause to *prior cause*, and thus onward through ascending causes up to God: " THE GREAT FIRST CAUSE." Thus it will appear that an *atom is created* by the concentration of particles of *eternal matter* having an *associative attractive affinity* for each other; and that a world is *created* by the concentration of *atoms* having an *associative attractive affinity* for each other; and that a solar system is *created* by the concentration of worlds having an *associative attractive affinity* for each other; and that a Universe is *created*, by the concentration of solar systems having an *associative attractive affinity* for each other; and that oceans upon oceans of universes are *created* by the concentration of universes having an *associative attractive affinity* for each other; and that the whole vast "UNIVER-SŒLUM" of matter is *created* by the concentration of *particles, atoms, worlds, systems, universes, and oceans upon oceans of universes* having an *associative attractive affinity* for each other; and that all this vast congregation of *forms of dense* and *rare* proportions, is but an expression of the *Divine Will* of that INFINITE INTELLIGENCE and rightly exalted SUPREME OMNIPOTENCE—GOD.

In this development we find that the gradually unfolding *form* is but the tangible evidence to our senses of an *interior cause or vital force*, the life-inspiring principle of matter, which, in its office, is simply refining, arranging, elevating, and *individualizing* eternal matter, which *individuality* eventuates in MAN, whose *interior Being* is denominated *spirit*, which spirit is in the precise "IMAGE" of its Creator, and in the order of eternal *progression is* refined, purified, and sublimated while *conditioned* in the flesh, and, when separated from the body, proceeds to a higher and a far more exalted state of Being, thus onward through ascending *conditions* up to God.

In this order of forms and things we find that the gross *cannot be made more gross*, but that the gross may be *refined*; and that, according to the laws of eternal progression it *must* continue to refine, however slowly and imperceptably to our senses, even though it be not demonstrable to our senses, yet, in the course of the infinitude of years it *will* be found to have advanced—progressed, and thence onward through the endless ages of *Eternal Time.*

From these deductions we *learn* that matter is *indestructable,* that its *divisibility* is infinite, that in reverting from one form to another it finally reverts to *positive motion, the vital force inherent in all matter.*

From the indestructability of matter it of necessity follows that nothing *dies*, that there is no such effect in nature as *death*, and that, when the interior or real reality of every *form* separates from the external, or, to our senses, *tangible* form, the external immediately falls into *decomposition* by the chemical action of the *vital forces* inherent in it, and by the action of the *same forces* the particles heretofore composing that form are carried into other *new* and *living* forms, thus onward through an endless series of *ascending forms* up to God; while the *interior* essence or real reality of the *same form*, at separation, by virtue of the *vital forces* inherent in it, *immediately ascend* to higher and more exalted spheres, peculiarly adapted to its continued progressive development, thus onward through ascending spheres up to God.

From these deductions it will be perceived that the whole *formula* of nature and *creation* is *composition, decomposition,* and *recomposition.* How simple, and yet how complex. For, unless we keep constantly in view the fact that *all forms* contain *within* themselves the *type* of the GOD-HEAD, or the *type* of MIND, MATTER, *and* MOTION ; in other words, and more especially when applied to *gross* forms, *positive* vital force, *negative* vital force, and matter ; in other words, *positive* magnetism, *negative* magnetism, and matter ; in other words, *positive* electricity, *negative* electricity, and matter ; and that these *three* forces are (for, when forms and substances are sufficiently *divided* they at once become *active, living* force,) in *essence One force, One vital* principle, *One mind;* ONE SUPREME INTELLIGENCE, thus unfolding the *Trinity* or *Type* of the GOD-HEAD in each and every form ; and, as the negative *is evolved from the positive,* so is *matter,* the *third element evolved from* the negative, thus establishing the *dual* character of the organic *Law,* its *attracting* and *repelling motions,* evolving *matter the third element* in all forms as the *result* of its motions, in the order of concentric circles, by the concentration of its own essence into particles and atoms, which are then *called* matter because *tangible* to our *senses,* which particles are then *transferred* by the action of positive and negative organic forces upon them, attracting and repelling each as the positive or negative may inhere in them, thus *creating forms* by the association of particles and atoms having an *attractive affinity* for each other, every atom of which form being *composed* of the essence of the vital forces inherent in it, which form, when thus created, evolves another *interior* form, similarly constituted, individual in its character, and is known by the appellations of *Instinct, Intellect,*

Mind, Reason, Spirit, thus becoming an entity—a *trinity* of vital forces, a *type* of the *Eternal* GOD-HEAD, which spiritual entity is of and unto Him, and whose *eternality* is in *His* express *" Image."*

Thus was and is the *creation of* MAN, who was and is evolved by *laws fixed and immutable as* GOD.

And thus were all things made that are made ; and thus was the Beginning ; for God spake and it stood fast ; *" the word was God."*

With this brief preface, the undersigned proposes to submit these writings to the people, not, of course, as conclusive proof of the theory herein set forth, but as approaching nearer the *truth* than the heretofore established theories extant in the world.

And further, he does not submit them as a continuous and elaborated argument, but simply as the *juttings or outcroppings* of a great system of ideas, thoughts, causes, and ultimates—the result of a penetrating analytic and synthetic research.

If, in these efforts he shall have elicited a new truth, or at least new to him and the world, and shall have elucidated others, he will be more than compensated for the many years of patient and laborious toil he has devoted to these inquiries.

Without desiring to provoke criticism or controversy, he most respectfully solicits for these brief writings a candid hearing, a careful examination, and if it shall be found that the basis on which this theory rests is erroneous, he will be among the first to discard it, as *his* sole object is the development of *truth.*

WASHINGTON, D. C., *August* 1, 1862.

HOME, NEAR BALLSTON SPA,
SARATOGA COUNTY, *New York, August 2d,* 1848.

DEAR SIR: I regret exceedingly the necessity of addressing you this note, but the importance I attach to the communication left with you for *publication some five weeks since* renders it actually necessary.

I care nothing about its publication, but wish to preserve a copy, and the reason of my not copying it was simply this, if you saw fit to publish it, I would retain a *printed* copy, if not, I would preserve the original.

I have no doubt you think it lost, but it must have been *mislaid,* perhaps in some drawer among your papers, and it may have been taken (by mistake) into the publishing office and laid away there. Suffice it to say, if you will (or can) find it and return it to me, I will pay you any reasonable sum you may demand for your trouble.

I esteem it of *vast importance to me,* and sincerely hope you may be fortunate enough to find it.

Your obedient servant,
GEORGE B. SIMPSON.

To T. G. YOUNG, Esq., *Editor, &c.*

HOME, NEAR BALLSTON SPA,
SARATOGA COUNTY, *New York, Sept. 5th* 1848.

DEAR SIR: Although I have *forgiven* you I cannot *forget* the *loss* of my communication.

The communication, considered as such, is of no account whatever. But this one contained the *key to a new order of things.* It opened the way and laid the foundation for the triumphant march of the mind of man to that high and exalted station designed by his Creator. It struck at the base of all error by bringing man forth according to fixed and unalterable *law, breathing through his nostrils "the breath of life," and receiving through his senses the spirit and impress of Deity;* when he was declared *perfect* and received the benediction of his Maker.

Then, having been brought forth according to *law,* which law constituted him a free (?) moral agent and held him amenable to its ordinances, he was then placed under another *law of rewards and punishments. This it is for which I grieve.*

It was the *result* of fifteen years hard study and investigation,

ing 10

and had I been worth fifteen thousand dollars and some one had told me I had lost the whole of it, it would not have produced a severer shock than when informed by you of the loss of my communication.

It is *truth* and the application of its principles to the utility of man which I am in quest of, and having wrought out what I considered the *true theory of man's creation and reduced it to a simple problem,* I ventured to lay it before the world. Judge of my surprise when informed of its loss. Nor can I give it up. And can only repeat my former promise that, if you will return it to me, I will give you any reasonable sum of money you may demand for your trouble.

This letter is not dictated in any spirit of anger but *grief.* As I am about to leave home, you will confer a lasting favor should you find the lost paper by returning it through the Post Office.

With great respect, your obedient servant,

GEORGE B. SIMPSON.

To T. G. YOUNG, Esq., *Editor, &c.,*
BALLSTON SPA, N. Y.

———

CAUSE AND CURE OF CHOLERA.

READING, PA., *May,* 1850.

DEAR SIR: As the season is fast approaching when the universally dreaded disease, "Cholera," is expected again to make its appearance in our midst, visiting alike all classes of the community, everwhelming the timid with fear, infusing death into the stoutest hearts, and spreading desolation in its wake; it may not be amiss to throw out some hints as to its probable cause and effect. From personal observation and investigation, I have determined it to be a nervous disease, operating directly on and through the sympathetic nerves. These nerves are the agents or conductors of animal heat, which is the cause of all sensation—the vitality of life; and they (the sympathetic nerves,) exist in every part of the physical organization. By some cause, the animal heat is thrown off, or extracted from the nervous system, when the sympathetic nerves become inactive, refusing to perform their natural functions. The thirty-two distinct sets of muscular nerves now lose their equilibrium, and being under the full force of muscular action, *contract,* without having the corresponding force to *expand.* This disorganizes the entire system, and an almost instantaneous prostration of the *man* must inevitably follow.

The animal heat being thrown off, one portion of the principal system becomes *inactive,* while the other remains in *full force;*

hence, indigestion, relaxation of the abdominal organs, purging, and coldness of the extremities, are its never-failing symptoms.

No matter which of these four symptoms appear first, they are all produced by the same cause, namely, the extraction of the animal heat—the vitality of life—the functionary power of the sympathetic nerves. Thus we infer the physical structure to be under the control of two forces analogous to each other, a positive and a negative; and in all "cholera" subjects, the positive being arrested and the negative remaining in full force, an unnatural, spasmodic convulsion must be the unavoidable result. In evidence of this hypothesis, witness the convulsions, spasms, purging, vomiting, and COLDNESS of the person, which not unfrequently equalizes the human body to the natural coldness of inanimate matter around it *before life is extinct!* Proving conclusively, in my opinion, the absence of all animal heat, and the consequent inaction of the sympathetic nerves, while the negative power is in full force, convulsing the system through the medium of the *muscular nerves.* Restore the *animal heat,* and you *balance* the corresponding forces, when the sympathetic nerves immediately resume their proper functions, hold in check the unrestrained power of the negative force, calming and quieting the muscular nerves, and tranquilizing the whole nervous system.

Without giving a physiological dissertation on the human system, I have ventured the above suggestions as the result of my experience.

Very respectfully,

VERASTUS.

To the Editor of the *Gazette & Democrat.*

HARRISBURG, Pa., *June,* 27, 1850.

DEAR SIR: On the eighth of this month your valuable Journal contained a communication from me on the *"Cause and Cure of Cholera."* The object of that communication was to assign a *cause* for that terrible disease, and suggest a probable remedy. That remedy, I am happy to inform you, has been discovered and successfully applied. Permit me to make an extract; it is taken from yesterday's Baltimore *Sun,* and is as follows:

"NEW CHOLERA CURE.—Dr. Macrae, in the Hospital at Howrah, has, according to the Indian *News,* discovered a new and most successful mode of treating Cholera patients. He causes them to inhale a certain quantity of oxygen gas, which contributes a strong stimulating effect, and finally throws the patient into a refreshing sleep. On awakening, he finds himself restored to health, with the exception of a general weakness which always succeeds every physical prostration. Dr. Macrac had tested his mode of practice upon fifteen European seamen, who had been carried to the Howrah hospital in the last stages of the disease, and the patient has in every instance recovered."

In my opinion, the above mode of treatment is the only effectual remedy ever applied to the disease; for if my theory be true, "the animal heat is thrown off, or extracted from the physical system," and there must be something to supply its place, or it is evident that the patient cannot recover.

The inhalation of oxygen gas seems to infuse itself into the sympathetic nerves, occupying the office made vacant by the extraction of the animal heat, sustaining the equilibrium of the two forces, and inducing the return of the positive force, or animal heat. How simple, and yet how effective. That there should be a certain, sure remedy for this terrible disease is perfectly natural, and that it is the inhalation of oxygen gas appears more probable than any other remedy ever before known. If this cure be a legitimate one, (and I firmly believe it is,) three years will not elapse before the Cholera will be classed among the standard diseases of the country, known, and curable at will; and carrying with it no more dread and terror than the "chills and fever," or "a slight cold."

With great respect,
Your obedient servant,
VERASTUS.

J. Lawrence Getz, *Editor Gazette & Democrat.*

———

(Another Communication from "Verastus" upon the Cholera question, has been received; but as we do not think a continuance of the controversy would be productive of any benefit to our readers, we beg respectfully to decline its publication.)

Harrisburg Pa., July 15, 1850.

Dear Sir: On the receipt of your valuable Journal this morning, I was agreeably surprised to find that my communications on the "*Cause and cure of Cholera,*" have attracted the attention of the "Medical Faculty."

Without any pretension to learning, science, or medicine, I offered those communications as the *result* of my "experience and investigation," believing, as I now most firmly do, that their theory rests on an *immoveable basis* and will stand the test of the most rigid *criticism.* The *dash* your learned correspondent made at that theory most effectually tore the mask from his own profession, and exposed to the gaze of enlightened minds, and in all its naked deformity, a ghastly "*skeleton*" of incomprehensible proportions, mystified by a tissue of physiological subtleties and technicalities, and proped up and supported by the "PRACTICE" of the Faculty from time immemorial. He whose mind is chained to books, is as effectually a *slave* as he whose hands are chained to labor. By attempting to combat a theory which he could not comprehend, your correspondent very modestly offers his services to "VERASTUS," as instructor of his "ignorance," and refers him to "authors" for information, who know not themselves the "*cause*" of the subject on which they treat. Permit me here to make an extract from an AMERICAN author, with whom, no doubt, your correspondent is quite as familiar as myself, and with whom we both agree.

"That fluid which exists in the sympathetic nerves, and which is the grand agent of transmitting all sensations to the brain, by means of the brain's magnetic power, is ANIMAL HEAT; and that fluid which moves the muscular nerves, through the exercise of the will, is ANIMAL ELECTRICITY." *Animal heat exists in the body: it is a subtle, sensitive fluid, and is confined to the sympathetic nerves, and extends through the whole animal economy. It exists only in animal bodies.* The vital functions are performed by this fluid; every involuntary secretion is made by it; every involuntary action of the system is carried on and propelled by *animal heat.* All impressions made upon the body are by this fluid unavoidably and irresistibly carried to the sensorium of the brain, through the attractive power of that organ; and every muscular action, as before stated, is performed through the exercise of the will, and by the aid of *animal electricity.* These are the agents of all voluntary and involuntary motions in the animal frame."

We have in this quotation the true theory of animate existence, which is governed by two laws or forces analogous to each other, and which are, in a modified form, the primitive organic laws of all matter whether animate or inanimate. Now, your correspondent stigmatizes the idea of the inhalation of oxygen gas and its consequent infusion into the sympathetic nerves, and in the very next breath declares the fact by the vaguest of all vague terms—"*absorbed by the blood!*" and gives the most convincing proof of *its* practicability and the truth of my theory. He says, "the same gass is inhaled by the lungs and absorbed by the blood." What is the blood? By what power is it forced through its avenues? This is the *only* medium by which an ulterior agent could be infused into the sympathetic nerves—"its inhalation by the lungs and absorption by the blood!" Here is the office made vacant by the extraction of the animal heat held in durance by the temporary occupancy of the oxygen gass, which exercises a corresponding influence over the *negative* or muscular force, inducing an immediate return of the *positive* force, or *animal* heat. This accomplished and the patient is restored to health.

As your correspondent has voluntarily proffered instruction in the science of medicine and physiology, I would respectfully ask him a few simple questions for information. Man has five external senses, (and one internal.) Has he more than one mind? If a bone be broken, will it grow together again? And why? If an incission be made in the flesh, will it heal again? Why? By giving a philosophical answer to the above questions he will impart information to one whose " glory's tarnished," and whose " occupation's gone, "(according to " Veridicus.")

With great respect,
Your obedient servant,
VERASTUS.

To J. Lawrence Getz, Esq.,
 Editor Gazette and Democrat, Reading, Pa.

This letter was returned by request—not published.

GEORGE B. SIMPSON.

Cincinnati, Ohio, *May* 10*th*, 1851.

Highly Esteemed Friend: Not only in accordance with my promise but inclination, I resume my pen to perform what is to me a pleasure, though fear I may fail to interest you.

Should my scribbling prove dull and incipid, or melancholy and sombre, attribute it to an overfondness for pensive reverie, or deep, lonely, silent thought.

Partly from habit, mostly from natural desire, I have acquired a taste, a passion for this species of meditation. It has often carried me beyond the bounds of propriety, and made me appear sedate, melancholy, cold, and passionless ; but the reverse is the case.

Generous, ardent, frank, and free,
I live to *love*, and love to *live* for thee:
My Mother.

Pardon me, my noble friend, for introducing this sacred name into this epistle, but as I *know* you love and reverence your mother, so also, I love and reverence my mother ; and an allusion to that name above all others in this world the most sacred, the name we both love to cherish, honor, and esteem,—*is our Mother* ; (God bless them,) and is therefore always pardonable.

My trip from Harrisburg to Hollidaysburg was pleasant, though the air was exceedingly chilly. I remained at Hollidaysburg five days, but no business opportunity offered itself for my acceptance. It is a beautiful place, situated in one of the most lovely rural districts in Pennsylvania.

On the south is a high hill bearing the name of "Chimney Rock," (it should be called *Monument Rock*,) from the fact that from its summit shoot up two monumental columns to the height of about sixty feet from their base, with an extended breastwork eastward of about forty feet high, thence sloping gradually to the waters of the "blue Juniatta." The "BURG" is situated in a basin, surrounded by elevated hills of about fifteen miles circuit. But, like most other towns in Pennsylvania, it is perfectly destitute of energy, public spirit, and, I almost said, individual enterprise, and the dirtiest place I ever saw.

On leaving Hollidaysburg, two ladies and two children were put into my especial charge to this city; my accustomed galantry would not allow me to decline the *fair* charge, however exceptionable the appendages might be. I helped the ladies in and out of the car, the carriage, and the boat; looked after their baggage, ordered the servants, and *nursed their babies.*

Methinks I hear you exclaim, how enviable! However, they were truly ladies, with whom I was much pleased, and, on arriving here, they tendered me their profound acknowledgments, with many thanks and the best of wishes. This more than paid me for any little trouble or inconvenience they may have put me to, and with characteristic frankness I remarked, "not at all ladies—you are under no obligations to me, if, by these courtesies and attention I have been of service to you while unprotected by any immediate gentleman friend, *I am doubly paid in knowing that I have performed but a small part of the great duty* I OWE MY MOTHER." All ladies, everywhere, when unprotected by gentlemen friends, have a *right*, and should demand the services of any *gentleman* who may be travelling in the same direction.

We parted with widely different feelings from those with which we met. Our trip over the mountains to Pittsburg, and even down the river to this city, was pleasant so far as society is concerned; but the weather was *most* disagreeable. The forrests in this vicinity were generally green, and the fruit trees in blossom; but the air was chill and piercing; and on the nights of the first and second of this month, frosts were sufficiently severe to kill nearly all the fruit. South, the corn, tobacco, and cotton crops are much injured. *I* succeeded in taking a violent cold, and the chills have been playing up and down my back with a perfect "looseness," irrespective of the threatnings of internal heat. Yesterday the weather began to soften and to day it is mild and balmy. The buddings of the Alanthus and other tender trees are T totally killed, and will have to regerminate or "loose the best of their time." Great improvements have been made in this city since I was here, with a great many valuable and important improvements now going on. This *is* the "Queen city of the West" may she win a crown of imperishable glory.

"The American Association for the advancement of Science" commenced its sessions in this city on Monday morning last, and closed its labors last evening; and, as you might naturally expect, your humble servant was a constant attendant.

I forwarded you a paper containing a vindication of Mitchell's genius and attainments, sanctioned by the highest scientific authority of America. The only applause manifested during the session was given while that paper was being read; a compliment richly merited and patiently won.

Much information of interest and importance to the general community was elicited, many hypothesises advanced, and new theories discussed. Geology occupied a large share of the time to the detriment of other sciences of quite as much importance.

Professor Peirce, of Harvard, advanced a *new* theory in regard to Saturn's Ring, which Professor Mitchell characterized as "*bold and startling*." He argued, that a *solid* could not be maintained either by the Primary or its satillites; that if the Ring be a *solid* it must oscillate, and its irregularities would bring it in contact with the primary, which would break it in pieces, the fragments form themselves into secondary planets and revolve in their respective spheres. From an analytical investigation he had ascertained the Ring to be *fluid*, of about the heft of water, every particle of which, however small, was a globe or planet of itself, held to and associated with the great mass by attraction, the whole flowing in streams or currents, in number from one to twenty, around the primary, constantly changing, and held in its position by the secondaries!

Truly, this is "bold and startling;" for if it be fluid, held in its orbit by the attractive force of the satillites, there is no reason why that force should not attract those particles or currents to those planets, and thus destroy the Ring altogether, associating with and becoming component parts of those vast bodies.

But, in my very humble opinion, the Ring is neither SOLID *nor* FLUID, *but* AIREFORM, *or* ELECTRICAL.

I shall assume the latter. The weight of the primary is estimated at that of cork or light wood, with an extreme rarified atmosphere, sustaining immense heat. This heat is reflected back from the surface of the planet to an immense distance, where the atmospheric gasses become nearly separated and pure, forming above them an electrical belt or zone encircling the planet, which, in form, volume, change of currents, and color, bear a strong resemblance to our light "arora borealis." This, in my very humble opinion, is the only theory on which the Rings of Saturn can be permanently based.

The same theory holds good in regard to all the other planets, especially the earth. The Sun being heat, or magnetism, becomes positive and attractive; the Earth being cold, or electrical, becomes negative aud repulsive; hence, we have the two laws of primitive order, organic in their strucrure, and infinite in their application. All suns or fixed stars are positive; all planets or opaque bodies are negative, revolving around the suns, and the secondaries re-volving around the larger planets by their borrowed heat from the primary suns.

To illustrate: the earth is many times larger than the moon, reflecting the heat of the sun; while the moon absorbs the sun's heat, it is attracted by the earth, and revolves in its orbit around that planet.

Methinks I see you tear this paper and hear you exclaim, "Dam" (this is Grace Greenwood's swearing) the fool! Very well; if it is too lengthy, too prosy, too incipid, or too assuming to meet your approbation and offensive to your good taste and superior judgment, please hand it over to my friend, Mrs. Joanna W. Hale; at any rate, permit her to read it. I know of nothing that would be of greater general interest to you, and if this should chance to meet your approbation, it will afford me much pleasure on a future occasion, to throw out some crude ideas that have suggested themselves to my mind in regard to the geo-logical features and magnetic influences of the earth's structure.

Receive my best regards. Remember me most respectfully to Mrs. Hale, Miss Joanna, Grand-mother Ramesey, Miss Cally, Miss Lena, the girls, Barnett, and especially your brother, and the members of your engineer corps. Adieu; write soon.

With high regard, your friend and obedient servant,

GEORGE B. SIMPSON.

To SAMUEL L. MORTON, Esq., Engineer, &c., Harrisburg, Pa.

INDEPENDENCE, MISSOURI, June 9, 1851.

To the Editors of the Occidental Messenger :

GENTLEMEN : There appeared in the last number of your jour-nal an article originally published in the North British Review, headed "THE DOOM OF THE WORLD." The author no doubt attempted to work on the fears and superstitions of the un-learned, that he might the more easily coerce them into a belief of his theory. He speaks of the internal fires of our own planet, the fragments of other planets wheeling their destructive elements at the solar surface, an influence, a subtle fluid, that is gradually

2

destroying the equilibrium of the gravitating forces, which must, some day, work the certain "*doom of the world.*"

Were it possible to conceive of a theory as utterly at variance with the true laws and principles of nature, as the one here put forth, we should certainly despair of an *object* for creation. Deity unquestionably *had* an object in the creation, that object we conceive to have been the production of a BEING who should glorify his creator, and to bring about this *designed* result, chaotic matter was placed under *law*. A positive and negative organic law proceeded directly from Deity, and all other natural laws are but modifications of these two.

All matter throughout the boundless universe of God, is subject to an immutable law of *change*; this change is but the process of creation, which is as effectually going on to-day as it was six thousand years ago. The positive organic law of creation inheres in the suns, the negative in the planets, hence the revolution of the latter around the former.

Now, can a planet come in contact with another planet, a planet with a sun, or a comet with either, without one of the organic laws being first destroyed? Impossible! Then, destroy either organic law, and not only all worlds, but systems and universes throughout infinity of space become a general wreck, enveloped in one universal conflagration—all matter reverting directly into its primitive chaotic state. If this be the case, what object in creation? Has it been attained? We might enlarge, but pause for an answer.   Respectfully,

GEORGE B. SIMPSON.

HOME NEAR BALLSTON SPA,

SARATOGA COUNTY, NEW YORK, *October* 19, 1853.

[Continuation of my Journal.]

Here, in the room where my mother died, familiar scenes, and things, and voices, bring vividly to mind the long lost past, and that most familiar of all voices, my mother's, rings sweetly in my ear—"*forgiven.*"

"My boy, the future is full of hope; life blooms with fresh vigor, and in thy honest poverty thou art rich in noble thoughts and generous sympathies, and the opening future will unfold to thee new beauties, fresh and blooming from the Edenic gardens of universal truth."

Thus she said, or seemed to say, and the spirit vanished.

BALLSTON SPA, SARATOGA COUNTY, N. Y., *October* 30, 1853.

To MRS. SEMANTHA METTLER :

MADAM : I have this moment read of your wonderful powers of psychometry, in the delineation of individual character by placing a piece of the person's writing on your forehead, and that "this is now a part of your profession."

This information I obtained from the "Shekinah," and my object is to obtain a delineation of the author's (of this note) character, and its adaptation to the affairs of life.

Name the amount of pay for your services, and I will forward it by return mail.

Very respectfully, your obedient servant,

GEORGE B. SIMPSON.

———

HARTFORD, CONN.; *November* 3, 1853.

PSYCHOMETRICAL PORTRAIT }
OF Mr. GEORGE B. SIMPSON. }

This is a person who possesses a *strong active mind.* He is ever searching into the depths of things, endeavoring to understand the hidden laws that govern not only his own nature, but all things that have an existence. *"Light, more light,"* seems to be his constant desire. His perceptive powers are quick and active, and his ideas are of a refined and elevated character, with much originality. Is always comparing and bringing up in his mind the analysis of things in general, and when he sees an effect, always desires to ascertain the cause. He is *benevolent* and *universal* in his feelings. It would be impossible for him to be an exclusive being at heart, if by *profession.* He venerates the good and true wherever found. He possesses a mind capable of defending himself. In contending for what he deems to be true, he would do it in a manner that would carry strong conviction. He loves that which is beautiful in nature or art. Has energy enough to acquire that which would add to his own comfort as *well* as others. He is polite and mannerly; has much suavity of manner; is attractive, and I should think would be likely to gain many friends and admirers. He is cautious in all business matters; exercises good judgment in whatever he is called upon to do. I should think him quite a *student of nature*; would love to repose. He has strong concentration; can speak or write forcibly. I should think he was very fond of his parents and his childhood's home; at times loves quietude, though I should think he would be likely to *tear* himself away from home for the purpose of seeing and knowing something of the world at large. To a child of his own he would be very affectionate and loving; might be somewhat inclined to idolize it. He is very fond of the society of ladies;

would be likely to make himself very agreeable in their presence. He has strong social affections; seems to be a person that can conform to almost any condition of life and be content. He is very orderly and punctual; is accurate in calculating; is exceedingly found of music, and delighted with everything that would tend to harmonize and elevate the character; the moral and intellectual faculties predominate, and the sphere is very agreeable."

The above is the original letter by and from Mrs. Semantha Mettler, wife of Dr. J. R. Mettler, of No. 8 College street, Hartford, Connecticut, and is, if I am any judge of myself, *true to nature*; and is inserted here as a *curiosity*.

I never saw either of these persons, and the only evidence *they* have of me is my letter to Mrs. Mettler soliciting an analysis of my "character and its adaptation to the affairs of life."

GEORGE B. SIMPSON.

NOVEMBER 19, 1853.

I discoursed to them on the sciences, the process of creation, the laws that govern matter, and the immaterialty (?) of things.

I hold that there is no such law or influence as *gravitation*; but *attraction*, and *repulsion*, and the *sphere of motion*.

DECEMBER 2-3, 1853.

This was an argument with a Presbyterian minister from Tennessee, covering seven pages of my diary, most of which is embodied in my letter published in the *Western Dispatch*, in 1854, under the title, "Is it so?" And was republished in the *National Intelligencer*, of Washington, D. C., in 1857, and is again republished in this series.

DECEMBER 5, 1853.

I suggested to him the great *idea* of the age, namely, the reduction of law, government, association, science, theology, and philosophy to the system of a *sphere*.

INDEPENDENCE, Missouri, January 1, 1854.

E. D. MANSFIELD, Esq.:

DEAR SIR: In your valuable *Railroad Record* of the 22d of December ultimo, I observe a notice taken from the London *Times*, of a *motion* claimed to be *perpetual!*

It will be no news to you, sir, when I assure you that *that* motion is yet a *mystery*.

Though some of the most valuable machines that now adorn the mechanic arts are the results of labored efforts to discover that hidden power, it still defies all research, slumbering securely in the deep infinitude of compound organic law.

Machines have been constructed which have moved themselves from one locality to another, indicating an *inherent force* to overcome atmospheric pressure and *propel inert matter*, but *friction*, incident to all mechanical movement, lessens the motive power according to the decay of material, both of which *must cease.* This, however, should not retard research, for a *perpetual motion exists, and that which exists in nature may be produced in art.*

Very respectfully, your obedient servant,

GEORGE B. SIMPSON.

[For the Western Dispatch.]

IS IT SO?

MR. EDITOR: If there was no Cause, there could be no Effect; therefore, inasmuch as the latter *is*, the former *must* have been, consequently, all effects revert immediately to a First Cause, from which we infer Matter to have existed with Deity, Nature and Revelation to have existed in harmony with each other, both in harmony and existent with Deity himself. Deity is a trinity of essences—Truth, Love, and Wisdom; from whom all truth, all love, and all intelligence emanate; and all existences, material or immaterial, are but the expressions of His will. Hence the object of Creation, which we conceive to have been a result that should glorify Himself. He is represented by the inspired penman to have reasoned with himself, saying: "Let us make man in our own image," &c. If this be true, then MAN was the *object* of creation, or a material essence so highly refined as to be capable of uniting with or *individualizing* spiritual essence, possessing, in degree, all the attributes of Deity, in conjunction with the appetites of a material organization. This material essence we find in the *mind* of man, and as all internal impressions must come from the external universe, it is reasonable to suppose that the five external senses were the medium through which was conveyed to the mind of man his spirituality, which is "in the precise *image* of his creator." And since it was the *design*, the *object* is accomplished in the production of a Material Immaterial Being, possessing all the attributes, in degree, of material and immaterial essence; hence it is the *perfection* of matter and the *individuality* of spirit. Mind, then, is the highest state of refinement to which matter is susceptible of being wrought—the perfection—epitome—result of creation, on which sits enthroned REASON. From this high eminence of mental and spiritual intercourse, the mind sweeps over the material universe, attracting to itself Truth and repelling

Error, analyzing matter, reducing compound natural law, giving cause to effect, design to cause, and Divinity to design. Inasmuch as the five external senses are the medium of conveying impressions from the external world to the mind, so, also, is a sympathetic nervous fluid the medium of conveying impressions from the internal or spiritual world to the mind, coming before the attribute of Reason like evidence before a judge, where it is arranged, condensed, decided on, and passed over to WILL for execution. As the mind *wills*, so the body *acts*. Consequently, internal impressions or thoughts are manifested by external signs. Having now shown Man to have been the *design* and *result* of creation; the union of matter with spirit; the operation of mind on matter, and the *supremacy* of Reason, we will now pass down through the great chain of existences to "chaotic" matter, and we find, from the highest Caucasian intellect and the most purely developed mentality, a uniform grade of animate existences, one above the other, according to the fineness of physical structure, each revolving in its peculiar sphere, and each reigning supreme over all inferior creation.

Now to the laws that govern: We can conceive of the existence of matter in an eternal state, but it is impossible to conceive of its creation out of *nothing*, for Deity himself is something, and if it emanated from him, it must have existed with him, therefore the "beginning was the word, which was God." The word was the Law, which "He spake, and it stood fast." After having *reasoned* with himself and determined to bring about a result that should glorify himself, he institutes, or establishes, Law, under which he passes "chaotic" matter. Law is limit, both simple and compound, and the "beginning" was when chaotic matter became subject to Law, and limited by a sphere; hence all law, all motion, is spherical. Motion was the *result* of Law; *change of particles* the result of motion; *globular forms* the result of the sphere. The organic laws are simple, being two, a *positive* and a *negative*, attracting and repelling each other; crude, "chaotic" matter now being subject to Law, became thoroughly imbued with it, every particle partaking of the nature of the law, becoming either positive or negative, acquiring polarity, and is attracted or repelled by one or the other of the two laws that may inhere in it. Law induces motion; motion induces change; change induces forms having an affinity of particles; forms induce concentration; concentration induces instinct; instinct induces intellect; intellect induces mind; mind induces spirit; spirit induces God, in whose attributes it will ever unfold in capacity to enjoy, never comprehending Him.

We have already shown that a law or force gravitating to the centre of all bodies does *not exist*, and in treating of a body that should fly off from this planet reaching a point in space where it can neither ascend, descend, or revolve on a plane, will further show the impossibility of such a law, such an effect. "The world was without form and void." This passage of the Mosaic record clearly shows "chaos" to have been an unshapen mass of molten matter, until it passed under organic law; as soon as it became subject to law, attraction and repulsion induced transition of particles, and the mass became instinct with motion! Motion marked its orbit, it revolved on its axis, and the "evening and the morning were the first day." The planet, for it has now assumed globular form, is encased in a dense volume of vapor, for the watery element at this time must have existed in vapor, while the solids seek adjustment by affinity of particles, attracting and repelling each other, until adjusted by and according to law. At this stage the commotion of elements must have surpassed conception. The negative force inheres in the planet, the positive inheres in the sun, consequently the earth is attracted by the sun, until its attraction is overcome by repulsion, when the planet again flies off from the sun, revolving in a sphere on a plane. The sun being positive, attracts all bodies to itself, and were it not for the negative inherent force of the planets, would absorb them; but, repulsion overcoming attraction, it can only retain them within its influence, each revolving in a sphere or an ellipse, according to its volume and negative inherent force. A sun and all planets revolving within its influence is a solar system, which also revolve in a sphere as a whole, so that no planet or system ever revolves *twice in precisely the same sphere*, but all revolve in harmony and unison with each other; hence the "music of the spheres." Where, now, is the law gravitating to the centre of all bodies? True, movable bodies are retained on the surface of the planet, not by gravitation, but by atmospheric pressure induced by *electrism!* consequently no body can fly off from its surface, and if it could, it would revolve in a sphere on a plane, according to its volume and negative inherent force, which shows that there is no point in space where matter can become stationary, so long as it is subject to organic law. Destroy the negative law, and all planets will rush into the suns and be consumed by those vast luminaries; the suns rush into each other, until the whole "UNIVERSŒLUM" becomes one vast conflagration. Destroy the positive law, and the suns will cool and break in shattered fragments; darkness brood over the infinitude of space; the very essence of Deity himself will chill—congeal—and mad, impulsive, unrestrained organic law will hurl the "vestiges of creation" fierce through space, breaking, bursting, desolating, until matter shall be destroyed, force exhausted, and hope, love, beauty, swallowed up in the universal wreck of worlds! A catastrophe so repulsive to the human mind cannot happen, for Divine law is not only infinite in application, but infinite in duration. Hope; even beams from the shadows of despair. Love; smiles amid the faded flowers. Beauty; lingers on the brow of sorrow. Truth; leads us to the portals of light, life, and immortality; glory be to Him who sitteth on the Throne and reigneth for ever and ever; amen.

Respectfully,   GEORGE B. SIMPSON.

January 15, 1854.

DELAWARE, Nebraska Territory, *January* 23, 1854.

DEAR FRIEND : I have perused and reperused with much attention the communication over your signature which appeared in the *Western Dispatch* of last week. I was really astonished and amazed at the able and concise manner in which you discussed this *new theory,* or at least *new and strange to me.* My astonishment did not arise, as you may imagine, from any want of confidence in your ability. No, far from any such idea; but the conclusive, and I may add, persuasive manner in which you *forced one even unwilling to admit that you were correct in your new theory,* was really astonishing.

If this theme of yours is the correct and proper one, your question as to *"Where now is the law gravitating to the centre of all bodies?" will remain forever unanswered—from this simple fact, that there can be none.*

"Movable matter, as you state, may only be retained upon the surface of the planet by atmospheric pressure induced by electrism!" The atmospheric pressure, I am aware, is very great to the cubic inch, but at the same time, I fear not sufficient to retain bodies, particularly very light ones, upon the surface of a planet, for instance, the earth, without some other exerting influence acting in unison and harmony with the atmosphere.

Undoubtedly, by destroying the negative inherent force of planets, the power of attraction of the suns remaining the same, they would all rush into those great luminaries and be destroyed, and the whole " UNIVERSŒLUM " become one vast conflagration, and the reverse would take place by destroying the positive law— the suns would cool and break in shattered fragments—the very essence of Deity himself would chill—a catastrophe too repulsive and awful for the human mind to contemplate would ensue; but this can never happen, for Divine law is infinite in application and duration, and He who wields the arm of power over the vast and numberless worlds which are in space contained is omniscient, omnipresent and all powerful, and in his mighty sway worlds and planets are regulated and moved with less exertion than we use in regulating a watch.

In this discussion, my friend, you will find opponents at every step, but this I know will neither deter or discourage one of your capacity. Text-books and authors of unsullied merit and world-renowned fame *will be cited in opposition to your theory*, but perseverance may surmount any and all obstacles.

In all your endeavors to expound, explain, or discover a *new theory, based upon truths and facts*, rest assured that you will always find a firm friend, a zealous advocate, and a determined supporter in your humble friend, the writer of this letter.

The evening is now far advanced, and I will close and retire, hoping soon to have the pleasure of the perusal of a letter in reply to this from your able pen, and with my best wishes for your health and future success in life, I remain as ever,

Your sincere friend,   B. D. CASTLEMAN.

To Mr. GEORGE B. SIMPSON, *Independence, Missouri.*

INDEPENDENCE, MISSOURI, *January 25, 1854.*

DEAR FRIEND : Your letter of the 23d ultimo, referring to an article of mine in the *Dispatch* of last week, this moment came to hand.

The very flattering manner in which you refer to that production, excites in my mind a *fear* lest there should be a *weak point* in it.

I am aware it strikes not only at, but strikes down, the foundation of established theories, and opens up to the inquiring mind a pathway of light, in which is *Truth* and eternal life.

It does not overleap but breaks through all barriers ; marching boldly forward to free life, free thought, and free act ; and, when rightly and thoroughly understood, will elevate the human race to that social condition wherein peace will flow as a river, and Nature's own religion will inspire the heart to universal praise, sweetening and alleviating the toils of life, the din of whose industrial harmony will be as an eternal echo! The way is now open, not to one, but to all men ; and if what is there set forth be true, then, there is nothing in the material or immaterial universe but TRUTH, the negative of which is ERROR, that sweet morsel we delight to roll under our tongue, because some *priest* has bid us do it.

The world is now burdened by taxation, even to groaning, not in support of the state, but the *priesthood ;* and if there is any power in *Truth*, God granting me life and strength, I will wield a force that will hurl them from their high places and consign them to that oblivion they so justly merit. How preposterous the idea that one man should ask another to *preach to* him and then offer *pay* for it; is it not tantamount to the *purchase* of salvation for a price? However, "*through the foolishness of preaching many shall be saved.*"

Now, open the great book of NATURE by the side of REVELA-TION, and invite all men to read for themselves—to analyze the *truths* of each on the principle of a positive and negative, truth and error, light and darkness, heat and cold, solid and fluid, male and female, thus onward *ad infinitum*; and then, on the principle of a *sphere*, let then analyze all *motion*, and the results enumerated in the article referred to will stand forth in all their beautiful proportions, gradually rising from one sphere to another, thus onward through ascending spheres up to God!

Have no fears in regard to *the law of gravitation, for it certainly does not exist. But that a positive and negative organic law are the basis of all motion and all individuality, may be clearly demonstrated.*

I may, at some future time, offer further evidence in support of my theory already advanced.

I will comply with your request, and shall be happy to hear from you at all times; will also anticipate your arrival here with pleasure.

With sentiments of high esteem, I am your friend and obedient servant, GEORGE B. SIMPSON.

To B. D. CASTLEMAN, Esq., *Delaware, Nebraska Territory.*

P. S.—The words "*priest*" and "*priesthood*" in this letter are intended to apply to the general practice of "*preaching*," and are used in no offensive sense whatever. All denominations should "*teach*;" this was the Divine command. G. B. S.

INDEPENDENCE, MISSOURI, *February* 23, 1854.

DEAR FRIEND: Your very kind letter of the 21st ultimo this moment came to hand, and in noticing its contents, I regret to find you laboring under a mistake in regard to the *intent* of my letter to you of the 25th of January last.

You seem to construe the purport of that letter to refer to your "*sincerity,*" whereas it refers expressly to the article in question, to wit: "*Lest there should be a weak point in it.*" Nothing could have been more foreign to my feelings and intentions than to have imputed insincerity to the expression of sentiments at once so frank, generous, and noble. The *fear* was excited in my mind "*Lest there should be a weak point in it,*" (the article referred to,) and, after having *convinced my friends* of the truth of my discovery, then, on an uncompromising analysis it should turn out, like

Sir Isaac Newton's, to be no discovery at all. It was this search-ing analysis I feared and had more especially in mind at the time, and not the remotest idea of imputing insincerity to your generous sentiments; for, how could I bear the ignominy, the reproaches of my friends, after my conclusions shall have been demonstrated by my opposers as being *incorrect?* However, on a more thorough examination of the whole subject, my fears have entirely subsided, and my mind settled down in the conviction that it is not only true, but that it rests securely on the immutability and eternality of the DIVINE INTELLIGENCE.

You are correct in regard to the accomplishment of my object; nor could I hope for a result so desirable, as all reformations are progressive in their nature and tendencies, and the most I can hope to attain during my life is the laying of a foundation on which future generations may erect a structure which shall embrace the world—the whole human race—and endure through all coming time.

Inasmuch as the *Positive* and *Negative* organic law of the material universe is the basis of all science, and their development the *result* of an analytical analysis of all material things and es-sences, it follows that these researches are unparalleled by human investigation.

For the *Preacher* I would substitute the Universal *Teacher*; and, as a commencement of the inculcation of *truth*, I would levy an injunction on the mother's *lips*, and seal them against all error, false impressions, deceitful promises, and tyrannical authority. I would impress the mother's smile on the infant's mind, and on its cheek imprint the kiss of loving kindness; and then direct the plastic mind in channels of innocence, purity, and truth, and govern by *attractive interest* and sympathy. Oh! what purity of heart and soul lies in the mother's lap! That germ of love and inno-cence, that bud of future hope and promise, that life eternal em-bodied in the flesh; and because, forsooth, "*it's mine,*" shall I rule it with a rod of iron? *Is that eternal spirit mine because be-gotten by my agency?* And does *right* inure in *me* to *will* its acts, to *prescribe* its pleasures and enjoyments? Methinks an adequate and appropriate answer to the foregoing questions is found in the reply of Jesus, when he said or inquired, "*Who is my Father, and who is my Mother; wist ye not that I must be about my Father's business?*"

I greatly fear the *natural* relations of parent and child are not properly understood. I would rear the child by *love*, and direct its tastes, habits, and appetites by *attractive interest*; happiness is then *at home*, and home is a foretaste of Heaven on earth; where harmony, love, and purity reign, error and impurity cannot dwell.

As the basis of the physical universe has been defined, I will

now give you the *ultimate* of all moral and intellectual research—
the universal human text, namely, CONVICTION OF TRUTH
IS CONVERSION TO GOD. Now I ask you, what, in the sense
of revelation, is conversion to God? Is it not the conviction of
the truth of Revelation? What else? Or what more can it mean?
Does it not follow, then, that all truth is *revealed?* And error
being the opposite of truth, may not the *origin of evil* have been
the *misconception of truth and the misuse of things?* If this be
true, how *easy* to be converted; *use* and not *abuse, receive* and
not *deceive,* are the essential incentives to right action. The acquisition of truth being the basis of all motive, all desire, and the
possession of which the inheritance to a crown of unfading glory
that passeth not away, eternal in the Heavens, rejoice and be glad.

Next in order will be the basis of Association, Government, and
Law; these I have also written out, as you may remember to have
heard me read from my papers, but, as it might tend rather to
bewilder than elucidate what I wish to develop, you will please
excuse me for not appending it to this desultory epistle.

My object is now to form an ASSOCIATION on a *natural* basis,
develop the harmony of human existence, and unfold the true
object of life.

I want a press through which I may be enabled to promulgate
these living truths, and pour them into the human heart like the
inhalations of earth's sweetest odors.

I fear I have now wearied your patience by taxing your mind
with too long a letter; if so, the absorbing interest I feel in the
unfolding of nature in all her beautiful proportions must be my
only apology.

With sentiments of high esteem, I am your friend and obedient
servant, GEORGE B. SIMPSON.

To B. D. CASTLEMAN, Esq., *Delaware, Nebraska Territory.*

AXIOMS.

Truth is the basis of all right reason.
The mind that dwells in truth *lives* in light.
Life is but the means unto an end; pursue it rightly.
Live for noble ends, for immortality, and for God: then you
    will live to some purpose, and your end will be glorious.
Knowledge is the beginning of wisdom.
Wisdom is a knowledge of all things human and divine.
Knowledge is acquired by adding little to little.
Aspire to the highest eminence of human excellence.
Youth is the time to lay a foundation for old age.
Let your chief corner-stone be TRUTH.

ORDER is a universal law of Nature.
Obedience to law is one of the first duties of Man.
The *calms* of life are more dangerous than its storms.
In a storm one looks for principle to which to *cling* :
In a *calm*, he is too apt to think the principle will cling to *him.*
Magnetism is the positive organic law of Nature.
Electricity is the negative organic law of Nature.
These *two* perform all the functions of creation.
Man and all inferior animate existences were *created* by laws
 ordained by Deity himself; investigate thoroughly.
The mind that dwells in *error* gropes in darkness.
Curiosity is the inmate of prisons.
Law is limit. The *senses* convey *ideas* to the mind, REASON
 defines their extent, and WILL executes their mandates.
Let *virtue* be thy motto, shield, and defense.
Perfect virtue is perfect happiness.
Twine the virtues around thy heart like a floral wreath.
Search for *Truth* and apply her precepts to thy use.
All *error must perish,* but *truth will live forever.*
The intellect should be developed and *beautified with truth.*
Enjoyment consists in the goodness of the heart.
VIRTUE will strew life's way with flowers :
PATIENCE will twine them into beautiful wreaths.
By patience we are enabled to *overcome great obstacles.*
That which appears *impossible* to-day may appear quite pos-
 sible to-morrow.

SELECTED.

" Virtue's the friend of life, the soul of health,
 The poor man's comfort, and the rich man's wealth."
Kindness begets kindness and love *wins* the heart.

LOVE.

What is love ? 'Tis a pleasurable emotion
 That sits, enthrones, encircles, fills,
 And compasses the whole heart ;
 'Tis life, 'tis immortality.
The birds sing sweetest when their hearts are warm with love.
INDEPENDENCE, MISSOURI, 1854.

CAUSE OF ALL CAUSE—GOD. RESULT OF ALL
CAUSES—MAN.

INDIVIDUALITY.

1. MAN exists as an *ultimate.*
2. MAN, when he *is*, is surrounded by *pre-existing* results.
3. MAN is *influenced* by causes unfolding *forms* over which he
has no control.

THE RIGHTS OF MAN.

INHERENT RIGHTS.

1. The right inheres in MAN to *live*.
2. The right inheres in MAN to *think*.
3. The right inheres in MAN to *act*.

ORDER OF RIGHTS.

1. MAN possesses *inherent* rights.
2. MAN may possess *acquired* rights.
3. MAN may possess *delegated* rights.

NATURE OF RIGHTS.

1. Right is an attribute inherent in the *nature* of the producing cause.
2. Right inheres in the *nature* of Man by the fiat to be.
3. Right is supreme—sacred—because *inherent*.

MOTION.

1. Motion is the *result* of Law.
2. Change of particles the *result* of Motion.
3. *Forms*, the *result of particles* having an *affinity* for each other.

LAW.

1. Law is *limit*.
2. Limit is *motion*, marked by a *sphere*.
3. Its results, *innumerable and illimitable* spheres.

MENTALITY.

1. Instinct is the *result* of highly *concentrated matter*.
2. Intellect—*mind* is the *result* of *instinct*.
3. Soul—*spirit* is the *result* of *mind*, an *eternal essence*, an attribute of the DIVINE MIND, in whose presence it is ever unfolding, loving, and *instinctively* worshipping "the all-pervading and rightly exalted Supreme Omnipotence."

It is evident from these deductions that every particle of matter, animate or inanimate, exists and unfolds in an appropriate sphere peculiarly adapted to its organization, in which sphere it is supremely free to exercise those functions which conduce to the unrestricted development of its interior essence.

An effect is the external expression of internal cause, evolved by motion through a series of ascending spheres.

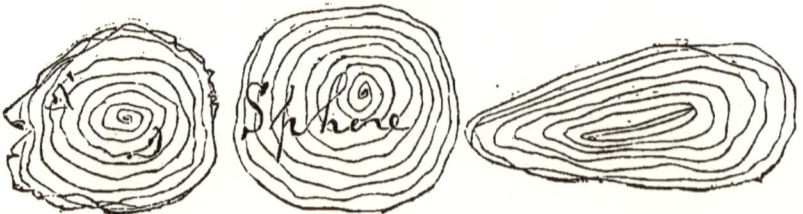

By this phrase we mean any form that has circular movement, whether concentric, elliptical, or spiral.

This is the order of Association :

1. Individual sphere.
2. Perfect enjoyment of all things *within* the sphere.
3. Association of spheres by attraction of mutual affinities.

This gives free life, free thought, free action, every one revolving *within* his or her own peculiar sphere, enjoying to the fullest and freest extent all things *within* that sphere, and associated with every other sphere beneath, around, above, by kindred ties of sympathy, interest, and society, evolving, in one eternal round of spheres, universal harmony, universal truth, universal love, universal justice, universal interest and association, peace unceasing, which is the universal brotherhood of Christ on earth, whose joys and rejoicings flow in strains of unmeasured harmony, echoing the songs of David and the sentiment of Him who said, "*Peace on earth, and good will to men.*"

This also gives natural life, natural association, natural religion, every one choosing his or her own sphere in life, objects of pursuit, and mode of worship.

This gives individuality to sphere, independent action and enjoyment within the sphere, and association of spheres by affinity of interests and social enjoyments.

The sphere is sacred, Divine, because it is an eternal order or law of nature, consequently all rights pertaining to a human Being are not only legitimate, but sacred, Divine, as is the internal essence their Being unfolds.

This unfolds the object of life ! which is the development of an eternal essence whose ultimate is Spirit, and whose office is " Glory to God in the highest."

This gives equality to right, for, if right inhere in me, it also inheres in you ; and if by my inherent rights I may acquire others, you may also acquire ; and if by my inherent and acquired rights I may attain to delegated rights, you may also attain ; and if my associated rights are sacred and inviolable, yours are equally sacred and inviolable ; and, as we cherish and esteem the sacredness and Divinity of our own rights, will we cherish and esteem the rights of others, for all are alike sacred, and of the same Divine Origin.

TRUTH is the primary and ultimate of all existences, whether material or immaterial, consequently *conviction of* TRUTH *is conversion to* GOD.

How natural the *conversion* when the Mind is once open to the *reception* of Truth.

REASON is the Divine attribute of intelligent Beings: *Truth* and *Reason* have such an affinity that it is impossible to prevent association when they come within the sphere of each other; consequently, it is only necessary to disrobe the Mind of preconceived prejudices, and unreservedly open it to the reception of all Truth, to become intelligent, learned, and wise.

Wisdom is the knowledge of Truth. Whether it flow to the mind in the unmeasured song of the mountain bird, enrupturing the soul with the harmony and melody of its music, or is borne on the breeze in the aromatic odor, or unfolds in the bloom of the flower, or is manifest in the blending of colors, the reproduction of kinds, the alternate change of seasons, the attractions of social intercourse, or the ecstatic joys of the wrapt soul that wafts on angel wings in imagination amid celestial spheres, all is alike Truth, the acquisition of which is knowledge, the constituent of wisdom.

How overwhelming is the contemplation of Truth! how sublime the idea! how glorious are its manifestations! and yet how simple. Truth! it exists in every *atom* of animated Nature; it is the essence of material and immaterial forms; it is the sublimity, the crowning glory of Reason. Sway thy scepter! O Reason! o'er the human mind; awake it to a living sense of the glory that surrounds it, that Truth may flow to it from unfolding causes, nourishing, vivifying, and imparting the living principle of light, life, and immortality. The mind that dwells in Truth *lives* in light. Light surrounds the throne of the mind by the emanating effulgence of Truth; Reason being the great arbiter of Right. How dignified, how just ought man to be? sitting, as it were, in judgment on his own acts, or, more properly, on those impressions made on the mind, flowing through his senses from external causes, over which he has no control. Although he cannot prevent the influx of impressions, he can, by the exercise of Reason, *reject* all that do not harmonize with Truth, Love, and Justice. Here is manifest the God-like attribute of man *in rejecting* the sensuous impressions of an animal nature, for, if there were no animal appetites craving indulgence to overcome, there could be no *virtue* in overcoming. What a gift! Reason to receive truth, and Reason to reject Error! How effectually are all sensuous impressions under the control of Reason! How unerring are all decisions, how exalted the judgment, how exact the justice, how pure, how holy the mind where Reason reigns supreme!

Impressions from the external world unbidden through the senses flow, and on the mind impress their image; some light, some dark, some black with crime,s most hideous forms—all *must* enter; but in the light of Reason darkness flees away, appetite and error are consumed, and Truth, beauty, and hope are mingled into love,

which is the essence of wisdom, the all-inspiring attribute of Praise.
Praise whom?

> "Praise God! from whom all blessings flow,
> Praise Him all creatures here below,
> Praise Him above ye heavenly host,"
> Praise God, praise Christ, praise Truth.

We cannot touch or behold an object, smell an odor, taste a substance, or hear a sound, without realizing Truth; it is the *"Alpha and Omega,"* the first and the last, the beginning and the end of all things. It is in the smallest *atom*, the simplest act, the grandest world, the sublimest thought; it lives, and moves, and has a Being in all material forms and essences, and in the spirit has a form unfolding into beauty and light ineffable, thus onward through ascending spheres of glory up to God!

Truth is in the frowning cloud, the lightning's vivid flash, the thunder's muttering roar, the whirling tempest, the devastating storm; it beams from the bright and living green of earth, the delicate inviting flower, the bud just opening into bloom, the pearly drop that hangs suspended from a blade of grass, the gentle zephyr, the sweet and stilly night, the playful twinkle of a star that floats in azure blue, and on the deep, deep blue of heaven is stamped the impress of eternal Truth.

> "Truth crushed to earth will rise again,
> The eternal years of God are hers,"

And in the temples where her light burned dim,
Will gleam the splendor of her radiant throne.
Those minds by error darkened will not slumber,
But when the light of Truth upon them flash,
Will waken to newness of life, and, like the mighty
Paul, exclaim, "What wilt thou have *me* to do?"
Believe! misguided soul, believe the *Truth* of *Nature,*
And from her *outward forms* receive the *evidence*
Of Truth *within,* which through the sense of feeling,
Sight, or sound, flows to the mind, where Reason
Dictates what to do, believe, embrace, adore!
Thy heart will never bleed, though *error die within it;*
For Truth, the *healing balm* of Gilead, will soothe,
Restore, imparting strength, vigor, life, light,
And glory ineffable where error reigned supreme.

INDEPENDENCE, *Missouri,* 1854.

INDEPENDENCE, MISSOURI, 1854.

There is a divinity *within* the human soul that moves man onward to noble deeds; it inspires with hope, and bids him *live.*
As if inspired with some superior power, man rises above him-

3

self, fixes his mind on high and holy aims, beholds the future, and *feels* as though ideal forms were types of what the real is to be.

Firmly impressed with the truth of what he *thinks* he sees, he braces himself against all danger, determined to press forward till victory shall crown his efforts, and his name is wreathed with living laurels of unfading glory.

This was the inspiration that moved Columbus to the discovery of a New World; it was this *divinity within the human soul* that moved Luther and Calvin against the Roman Church; it led Napoleon and Wellington to the battle-field of Waterloo; it filled the Pilgrim Fathers with hope; it gave confidence and courage to Adams, Hancock, Franklin, and their compatriots; it played around the heart of the youthful Washington as ideal Liberty flitted before his mind, and as the outlines of her graceful form became more marked and distinct, he *thought he saw* new charms, new graces, new beauties, and receiving new impulses from the innate power of inspiring causes; he looked again, above, below, beyond the gathering storm and actually *saw the real form of Liberty!* Fired with enthusiasm, flushed with confidence and hope, he believed the real would yet be his, and with a high, fixed, unalterable resolve, he marshaled his little army against opposing hosts, and led them on to victory! LIBERTY perched on the standard of inalienable rights, man rose to an equality with man, *power flowed from the people*, and the name of Washington impressed itself on every heart, surrounded by a halo of imperishable glory.

HEAT IN THE UPPER STRATUM OF A CLOUD.

————————, *December* 13, 1854.

EDITOR OF THE ——— ——— :

SIR: There appeared in the columns of your paper, a few weeks since, a brief account of of an aironautical tour, in which the aironautist experienced singular phenomena while passing through a cloud, the cause of which he desired to know. Without presuming that which I shall say is absolutely true, I may, with your permission, offer such suggestions in explanation as appear to my mind most probable.

If we take Sir Isaac Newton's analysis of the sun's rays as a guide, we must infer that the rays producing heat and chemical effects are intercepted by the vapor, the ray of light being more subtle, penetrates the mass by its inconceivable refractions, faintly illuminating the spot of earth shaded by the intervening cloud. Consequently, in penetrating the cloud upward, as in balloon ascensions, the lower stratum of the cloud will be conceivably colder than the surface strata of the earth's atmosphere, from the absence of the two rays and the emission of heat from the earth ; and the upper stratum of the cloud will be conceivably warmer, from the interception of the rays producing *heat* and chemical effects in combination with the ray of light.

Very respectfully,

GEORGE B. SIMPSON.

MAY 6, 1854.

In revolving in thought the probable order of the earth's strata, it occurred to my mind that the most condensed particle of matter sought the lowest and the rarest the most distant point in a sphere, and that each strata from the centre was formed in accordance with this law; if this be true, then indeed are we living "*in*" the earth as effectually as is the rock which lies embedded beneath its soil; for the hardened crust is but a sublimated strata of the liquid fiery centre ; the granite, mineral, and vegetable being in regular order, from which flows the watery element, then the atmosphere, *in* which "we live, and move, and have our Being;" beyond which is oxygen, flourine, and electricity in continued order of development, the latter being the outer and most sublimated strata of the earth's atmosphere, extending beyond and embracing the moon's orbicular movements.

This furnishes a rational explanation of the moon's running "*high*" and "*low*," showing conclusively that the moon is attracted north or south, as the case may be, by the passage of immense volumes of electricity from one pole to the other, thus acting as the earth's *Barometer*, and thus accounting for all the "signs" attributed to that body.

This shows that the moon has *no* influence on the earth, but the changes and "signs" of the moon, its supposed effect on the *tides*, atmosphere and temperature, are all directly traceable to the variations in the earth's electric envelope.

This also shows that if the earth could be enveloped in a network of metallic wire suspended in the atmosphere, the superabundant electricity would be conducted to the earth, thus restoring and maintaining an electric equilibrium and a more uniform atmospheric temperature.

This might also have a very beneficial effect on atmospheric diseases of the human, animal, and vegetable organisms.

Lightnings, whirlwinds, and devastating tornadoes would be prevented or greatly modified, thus securing life and property against the evil effects of a restoration of the unequally-distributed elements. *Law is limit.*

MAY 9, 1854.

Reflecting on the cause of the petrifaction of vegetable, flesh, and bone substances, it occurred to my mind that the chemical property or essence producing that effect resides *in* and is an inherent element of lime, or lime formations.

It also occurred to my mind that this peculiar property might be discovered by analyzing the water which leaches through lime deposits, where petrified fossils are discovered.

The discovery of this solidifying and stone-creating element, in its application to the uses of man, would be of greater value than almost any other discovery.

I have in my possession the flesh portion of a human body perfectly petrified, also the foot of an animal, apparently a buffalo, (after the hoof had dropped off,) both of which are in a state of perfect preservation, except the stony condition, and were collected with other fossils on Mount Adams, directly north of the city of Cincinnati, Ohio, in the fall of 1847.

It would appear that an immersion of the flesh, bone, and vegetable in this chemical solution interposes an immediate check towards decomposition, infusing itself into every pore and avenue of the substance immersed, till it becomes perfectly saturated with the chemical properties of the stone-creating principle of lime.

This may appear strange to many scientific minds; nevertheless it approaches near the truth, and may lead to a valuable and important discovery.

NOVEMBER 6, 1854.

CREATION is the development of *Forms* and the individualization of *Motion*, unfolded by the harmonious action of a positive and negative organic law.

LIGHTNING is the instantaneous expansion of highly concentrated matter, in the form of hydrogen gas, which is generated by the decomposition of water in the air, chemically acted on by heat and cold, or magnetism and electricity.

The earth's stratification is on the principle of a sphere, according to density and rarity of particles, the densest assuming the lowest, and the rarest the most distant point in the sphere, which shows that matter has but *two* conditions, *dense* and *rare*. This annihilates the *law* of gravitation, for, when a solid is reduced to rare, instead of "*gravitating*" in obedience to *the law* towards the *centre* of the planet, it *descends* upward to a strata of its own peculiar rarity.

This places man in the *centre* of the earth's strata, being unfolded in *form* between the solid and rarified strata.

Evaporation is caused by the positive action of heat upon cold;

in other words, the earth's electricity is repelled by the sun's magnetism, carrying with it into the upper regions infinite globules of
water, which associate and *form* cloud, and which, on further condensation, become too weighty to be borne up longer by the electric force, fall back upon the solid earth in the *form* of rain, snow,
and hail, seeking a strata of the same density.

In fair weather, those globules of water not associated into
cloud, after the going down of the sun, return to the earth again in
the *form* of *dew*, unless the emission of heat from the earth's surface is so great as to keep them suspended in the atmosphere.

The moon has no perceptible influence on the earth, being a
fragment of it, and revolves in its own orbit *within* the earth's
atmosphere; and, instead of causing the *tides* and atmospheric
changes, is itself acted on by the earth's electric currents, becoming, as it were, the earth's *barometer*.

Though these "*signs*" are attributed to the influence of the
moon, it manifests only the *effect*, the *cause* existing in the *variableness* of the earth's electric envelope. Therefore the "*signs*"
may be true, the cause never.

NOVEMBER 14, 1854.

In descanting on science and philosophy, I held that the tides,
wind currents, ocean currents, and "signs" of the weather, are
all attributable to the influence of the earth's electric and dia-elec-
tric currents. That all matter is subject to, controled, and unfolded by a positive and negative organic law; that it applies to
all material and *supposed* immaterial forms, and that *spirit* is but
the perfection and *individualization* of *motion*.

In morals there is nothing pure and eternal but *Truth*; there
is nothing mortal and perishable but *Error*; that "*Sin*" has its
origin in the misconception of truth, and the consequent misap-
plication of things.

Again, mind, muscles, members, functions, and fluidic forces are
all dual, and that man is simply passive in the development and
perfection of the internal or spiritual Being, his external being
acted on by ulterior forces over which he can exercise no control,
though ever *appearing* to choose for himself in the exercise of his
agency or functions, from the fact that the *superior* interests,
social and pecuniary, *force his will of the thing chosen*.

The Doctor (H. R. Wirtz, Assistant Surgeon United States
Army) admitted that there was an indescribable something in the
governing forces of the Universe not rightly understood.

In my opinion, there is one God, one Nature, one Law, one
Science, one Philosophy, one Religion or mode of worship, one

Eternity of duration, and one Infinite and eternal source of causation.

How futile the attempts of those who would establish a belief in a supernatural power or agency, weaving simple truths into metaphysical mysteries, bewildering the mind of the searcher after truth, and closing the door of nature's great labaratory to those who running might read and be guided by *her* simple truths.

But the day is passed; the dawning of a new era appears in the East; man is awakening from his long night of sleep to enjoy the light of truth, and breathe the sweetness of the fragrance she instills, and plant new flowers by the wayside for the youth of future ages to gather in their pilgrimage through life. Ay, the intellect of Man shall bud and blossom as the rose, till every thought shall be fragrant with some new and living truth, and every word shall be as the germ of a new thought.

How beautiful will then be the intellectual garden of life; how pure and holy its social relations; how sweet and enchanting its melodious music; how delicate the texture of every thought, word, and action; how high and ennobling the society of man! Is there not something in all this more than mortal? Is it not the divinely instituted attribute of *Reason*, which is of and unto the great DEITY! I think so.

PORTLAND, OREGON TERRITORY, *August* 3, 1856.

Mrs. WILLIAM HOLMES, *Oregon City, O. T:*

MADAM: In compliance with your wish, it affords me the greatest pleasure to offer for your acceptance the accompanying specimen of natural curiosity. This specimen possesses in itself no intrinsic value, and is esteemed only for its *display of mysterious forces.* In it are hidden the *organic laws* of matter, which are made manifest to our senses by placing bars of steel in juxtaposition to it, the mysterious forces attracting or repelling the bars of steel according to polarity. These forces are called *positive* and *negative*, and are the *active agents* in the development of all *material Forms.* They cause the blade of grass to shoot forth, the flower to unfold, give variety and color to its leaves, and throw off its fragrance.

They give power and vitality to the animal, unfold and perfect the human, and by their attractive influence cause the spirit to bloom in immortal glory. Look upon this cold and forbidding *Form,* pour over its unfolded pages and its hidden power, till from the depth of thought the mind becomes weary, or in its ascent it becomes dizzy from its towering flight; then, throw it (the mind) out into space, around, above, below, till it again becomes weary of travel, then recall it, place it again upon this dark cold rock, and ask, whence thy *origin?* what thy *inherent* properties? from whom emanates thy mysterious power? *The answer cometh not.*

Flattering myself that you will accept this little gift, not for its value in dollars and cents, but as a memento of him who has been blessed by your kindness, and the high esteem in which he now and ever holds you, your husband, and your family, he will feel himself obliged.

I have the pleasure to remain your friend and obedient servant,
GEORGE B. SIMPSON.

WASHINGTON, *April* 15, 1857.

To the Editors of the National Intelligencer:

GENTLEMEN: By the politeness of a friend I am permitted to copy the following extract from a private letter dated St. Louis, Missouri, November 9, 1856, which, for its direct bearing on a question now agitating the public mind, especially in Europe, I hope you will favor with a place in your columns:

THE PREDICTED COMET.

"Now, by way of fortifying your mind against fear, permit me to remind you that astronomers throughout the world are at this time looking for the reappearance of HEALLY'S great comet of 1765. The near approach of this planet in embryo will influence our planet, perhaps the entire solar system. It will be attracted by the sun, and then repelled by it; it will both attract and repel the planets of the solar system, and *appear* to create disorder—confusion. But have no fears. *It can neither attract nor be attracted so as to come in contact with any of the heavenly bodies.* The *most* it can do to any of the planets (ours not excepted) will be to *change the currents* of their electrical envelopes! This will have a tendency to give us the warmest or the coldest winter (should the comet appear soon) experienced since 1765. Should the earth's electricity be attracted or repelled to either pole, the temperate zones will enjoy an unusual degree of mildness; on the other hand, should the earth's electric sheen be gathered in folds nearing the equatorial regions, then indeed may we expect the most intense cold ever experienced in this climate. In either event the *disturbance* of the ocean of electricity in which the solar system floats will produce extraordinary results in atmospheric temperature, wind currents, and vegetation, until the electric equilibrium shall be re-established. This may appear strange to you, but by referring to an article of mine published in the *Western Dispatch*, of Independence, Missouri, in the winter of 1853-4, headed 'Is it So?' (which paper I think is in your possession,) you will not fail to observe the *cause* of the phenomena suggested above. These truths are important."

The foregoing suggestions may throw some light on the severity of the last winter and the backwardness of the spring.

Very respectfully, VERASTUS.

WASHINGTON, *April* 27, 1857.

To the Editors of the National Intelligencer :

GENTLEMEN : The letter referred to in my note of the 15th ultimo, and published in your paper of the 17th, is herewith submitted for publication.

By a careful perusal of this letter, it will be perceived that a comet is the nucleus of an embryo planet, and that it can neither come in contact with the central body of our solar system or any of its satellites.

The positive or negative organic law must first be destroyed, in which event the universe becomes one common wreck. No fears need be entertained of a collision with our planet; all it can do is to disturb the equilibrium of its electrical envelope.

Yours, very truly, VERASTUS.

[From the Western Dispatch.]

IS IT SO?—If there was no Cause, there could be no Effect; therefore, inasmuch as the latter *is*, the former *must* have been, consequently, all effects revert immediately to a First Cause, from which we infer Matter to have existed with Deity, Nature and Revelation to have existed in harmony with each other, both in harmony and existent with Deity himself. Deity is a trinity of essences—Truth, Love, and Wisdom; from whom all truth, all love, and all intelligence emanate; and all existences, material or immaterial, are but the expressions of His will. Hence the object of Creation, which we conceive to have been a result that should glorify Himself. He is represented by the inspired penman to have reasoned with himself, saying: "Let us make man in our own image," &c. If this be true, then MAN was the *object* of creation, or a material essence so highly refined as to be capable of uniting with or *individualizing* spiritual essence, possessing, in degree, all the attributes of Deity, in conjunction with the appetites of a material organization. This material essence we find in the *mind* of man, and as all internal impressions must come from the external universe, it is reasonable to suppose that the five external senses were the medium through which was conveyed to the mind of man his spirituality, which is " in the precise *image* of his creator." And since it was the *design*, the *object* is accomplished

in the production of a Material Immaterial Being, possessing all
the attributes, in degree, of material and immaterial essence ; hence
it is the *perfection* of matter and the *individuality* of spirit. Mind,
then, is the highest state of refinement to which matter is susceptible of being wrought—the perfection—epitome—result of creation, on which sits enthroned REASON. From this high eminence of mental and spiritual intercourse, the mind sweeps over
the material universe, attracting to itself Truth and repelling
Error, analyzing matter, reducing compound natural law, giving
cause to effect, design to cause, and Divinity to design. Inasmuch
as the five external senses are the medium of conveying impressions from the external world to the mind, so, also, is a sympathetic nervous fluid the medium of conveying impressions from the
internal or spiritual world to the mind, coming before the attribute of Reason like evidence before a judge, where it is arranged,
condensed, decided on, and passed over to WILL for execution. As
the mind *wills*, so the body *acts*. Consequently, internal impressions or thoughts are manifested by external signs. Having now
shown Man to have been the *design* and *result* of creation ; the
union of matter with spirit ; the operation of mind on matter, and
the *supremacy* of Reason, we will now pass down through the great
chain of existences to " chaotic " matter, and we find, from the
highest Caucasian intellect and the most purely developed mentality, a uniform grade of animate existences, one above the other,
according to the fineness of physical structure, each revolving in
its peculiar sphere, and each reigning supreme over all inferior
creation.

Now to the laws that govern : We can conceive of the existence
of matter in an eternal state, but it is impossible to conceive of
its creation out of *nothing*, for Deity himself is something, and if
it emanated from him, it must have existed with him, therefore the
" beginning was the word, which was God." The word was the
Law, which " He spake, and it stood fast." After having *reasoned* with himself and determined to bring about a result that
should glorify himself, he institutes, or establishes, Law, under
which he passes " chaotic" matter. Law is limit, both simple and
compound, and the " beginning " was when chaotic matter became
subject to Law, and limited by a sphere ; hence all law, all motion, is spherical. Motion was the *result* of Law ; *change of particles* the result of motion ; *globular forms* the result of the sphere.
The organic laws are simple, being two, a *positive* and a *negative*,
attracting and repelling each other ; crude, " chaotic " matter
now being subject to Law, became thoroughly imbued with it,
every particle partaking of the nature of the law, becoming either
positive or negative, acquiring polarity, and is attracted or repelled
by one or the other of the two laws that may inhere in it. Law

induces motion; motion induces change; change induces forms
having an affinity of particles; forms induce concentration; concentration induces instinct; instinct induces intellect; intellect
induces mind; mind induces spirit; spirit induces God, in whose
attributes it will ever unfold in capacity to enjoy, never comprehending Him.

We have already shown that a law or force gravitating to the
centre of all bodies does *not exist*, and in treating of a body that
should fly off from this planet reaching a point in space where it
can neither ascend, descend, or revolve on a plane, will further
show the impossibility of such a law, such an effect. "The world
was without form and void." This passage of the Mosaic record
clearly shows "chaos" to have been an unshapen mass of molten
matter, until it passed under organic law; as soon as it became
subject to law, attraction and repulsion induced transition of particles, and the mass became instinct with motion! Motion marked
its orbit, it revolved on its axis, and the "evening and the morning were the first day." The planet, for it has now assumed
globular form, is encased in a dense volume of vapor, for the watery
element at this time must have existed in vapor, while the solids
seek adjustment by affinity of particles, attracting and repelling
each other, until adjusted by and according to law. At this stage
the commotion of elements must have surpassed conception. The
negative force inheres in the planet, the positive inheres in the
sun, consequently the earth is attracted by the sun, until its attraction is overcome by repulsion, when the planet again flies off
from the sun, revolving in a sphere on a plane. The sun being
positive, attracts all bodies to itself, and were it not for the negative inherent force of the planets, would absorb them; but, repulsion overcoming attraction, it can only retain them within its
influence, each revolving in a sphere or an ellipse, according to its
volume and negative inherent force. A sun and all planets revolving within its influence is a solar system, which also revolve
in a sphere as a whole, so that no planet or system ever revolves
twice in precisely the same sphere, but all revolve in harmony and
unison with each other; hence the "music of the spheres." Where,
now, is the law gravitating to the centre of all bodies? True,
movable bodies are retained on the surface of the planet, not by
gravitation, but by atmospheric pressure induced by *electrism!*
consequently no body can fly off from its surface, and if it could,
it would revolve in a sphere on a plane, according to its volume
and negative inherent force, which shows that there is no point in
space where matter can become stationary, so long as it is subject
to organic law. Destroy the negative law, and all planets will
rush into the suns and be consumed by those vast luminaries; the
suns rush into each other, until the whole "UNIVERSŒLUM" be-

comes one vast conflagration. Destroy the positive law, and the suns will cool and break in shattered fragments; darkness brood over the infinitude of space; the very essence of Deity himself will chill—congeal—and mad, impulsive, unrestrained organic law will hurl the "vestiges of creation" fierce through space, breaking, bursting, desolating, until matter shall be destroyed, force exhausted, and hope, love, beauty, swallowed up in the oblivion of the universal wreck of worlds! A catastrophe so repulsive to the human mind cannot happen, for Divine law is not only infinite in application, but infinite in duration. Hope; even beams from the shadows of despair. Love; smiles amid the faded flowers. Beauty; lingers on the brow of sorrow. Truth; leads us to the portals of light, life, and immortality; glory be to Him who sitteth on the Throne and reigneth for ever and ever; amen.

Respectfully,   CITETUS.

January 15, 1854.

THE COMETS.

WASHINGTON, *May* 1, 1857.

To the Editors of the National Intelligencer:

GENTLEMEN: There is a divinity *within* the human soul that moves man onward to noble deeds; it inspires with hope, and bids him live. It was this divinity that inspired those illustrious benefactors of our race whose names are handed down to us as mementoes of the past, and which serve as beacon-lights to guide us in our onward march of progress.

Fron the days of Aristotle to the present time, philosophy and science have moved forward with a steady and unfaltering step, joined hand and hand, wedded together for all time to come. Philosophy called men from their isolated solitude and nomadic forms of life to that higher and more exalted sphere of association, and congregated them into communities, cities, states, and nations; instituting government, and giving laws that should guide their reason, govern their actions, and distinguish them from the lower order of creation. Science mounted his prancing steed and marshaled his eccentric few to battle against the superstitions of the Old World; he unfurled a banner to the gaze of men on which was inscribed, *Test shall establish the Truth.* From this the brave took courage, and Galileo, a philosopher, in opposition to the *established* theories of past ages and in defiance of inhuman persecution, proclaimed to men, "The earth revolves upon its axis!" Harvey also declared, "The blood circulates through the veins;" Sir Isaac Newton discovered what he termed "the law of gravitation, or a force tending to the centre of all bodies;" Columbus discovered a New World; Faust discovered the art of printing; Fulton discovered the art of applying steam to locomotion ; Franklin caught the electric spark, and Morse made it *tell*-egraph.

Thus we see, while philosophy has humanized, nationalized, and Christianized a very large portion of the human race, science has unfolded the laws that govern all organic and inorganic forms, which enables man at the present day to understand all the varied phenomena of nature.

Now, we will endeavor to illustrate, briefly, the rotary movement of solar bodies, and show the impossibility of a collision of our earth with a COMET.

The sun is the centre of our solar system, which has thrown off from itself the planets that revolve around it, whose atmosphere extends to the farthest verge of the orbit of a yet undiscovered planet, and whose rays vivify and impart life to all material forms. The positive organic law of matter inheres in the sun, and is magnetism or *heat*; the negative organic law of matter inheres in the planets, and is electricity or *cold*; consequently, attraction and repulsion become the manifest mediums of motion, which, when the sun's attraction is overcome by the planet's repulsive force, the planet shoots past him with accelerated motion, lessening in velocity, however, till the negative is again overcome by the positive, and the planet moves gradually towards the sun again, thus revolving in an ellipse, on a plane, forming a variable spherical movement. Therefore, all the planets are held in their orbits by the attractive influence of the sun, all are carried with that luminary, because they are of it and are within its atmosphere, thus constituting one body of dense and rare proportions, revolving around some other mighty and unimaginable centre.

It is now manifest that matter has but two conditions, namely, dense and rare ; and that motion is its actuating principle.

A comet is a negative body, a planet in embryo, whose nucleus is formed by the condensation of particles having an affinity for each other, which particles are gathered from the suns through whose atmosphere it passes, increasing in volume and density as it traverses space in an undefined sphere, until its dimensions determine its orbit, when it wheels into line and assumes position among the stars that stud the vault of heaven. While in the embryo state its electric envelope becomes luminous, constituting the "tail" that always *follows* the nebula as it approaches the sun, and always precedes or partially precedes it when receding from the sun ; thus showing conclusively that the comet is both attracted and repelled by the sun, as, for instance, when it has reached its perihelion and shoots past or commences to recede from that luminary, its "tail" or volume of electric vapor is thrown back upon itself by the repulsive force of the sun, entirely enveloping the nebula and forcing at least a portion of its former "tail" in advance of it. Now, while it is flying apparently at random through the solar system, may it not come in contact with a planet? No; such an effect is equally impossible, inasmuch as the luminous atmosphere of the comet contains a greater amount of *heat* than the planets; it will, when within a certain distanc , be repelled by every planet, shooting past them, though not without disturbing their electrical envelopes. *The electric pulsations of our own planet, as well as the volume of electricity enveloping a comet may be determined by mechanical experiment.* The appearance of two small comets in the northwest heavens in March and May of the present year is evidence to my mind that the earth's electric equilibrium is now disturbed, causing the unusually cold weather and backwardness of the spring, which will continue till the comets have passed by and the equilibrium is re-established; but that either will come in contact with the earth in June, or at any other period, is highly improbable, unless, indeed, the *positive* or *negative* inherent law of matter be first destroyed. This will be tantamount to the annihilation of Deity himself.

In another communication I will explain the *cause* of atmospheric temperature, the "signs," and show that the moon is simply the earth's barometer: that electric variations affect the tides, vegetation, and health.

Yours, very truly,   CITETUS.

THE MOON BAROMETER TO THE EARTH.

WASHINGTON, May 13, 1857.

To the Editors of the National Intelligencer:

GENTHEMEN : Having previously shown that *forms* are the only tangible evidences of creation, explained the origin of comets and the rotary movements of planets, we will now attempt to show that the moon is simply the *indicator* of the earth's electric changes, and that the moon itself has no appreciable effect upon this planet.

The moon is a fragment of the earth, is negative to it, and revolves upon its own axis *within* the earth's atmosphere.

The earth is enveloped in an ocean of electric vapor, dense and compound upon its solid surface, whose gases separate, however, as they deepen outward, the rare always emanating from and resting on the more dense, until we reach in outward order flourine, electricity, and magnetism, that subtle element pervading all space. Observing the various atmospheric strata above and the solid strata below us, it is not difficult to perceive that men, animals, and vegetable forms are existing in the *centre* of the earth's stratification.

The electric lines of no variation are those extending from the north to the south pole: the dia magnetic or dia electric lines are those extending around the earth from west to east, *and are ever variable.* It is the variableness of these dia electric currents that produce all the phenomena attributed to the influence of the moon upon the earth. "The moon runs high and is a *sign* of cold weather." This common popular phrase may be rendered thus: the moon is simply attracted by the earth's electricity towards the north pole, "runs high," and is said to be the cause of cold, storm, wind, &c., whereas, on the contrary, it is the great volume of electricity intervening between us and it, (the moon,) intercepting the *heat* of the sun's rays, producing cold, storm, wind, and a silvery gray atmosphere. "The moon runs low and is a *sign* of warm weather;" which popular phrase may be rendered thus: the moon is attracted by the earth's electricity towards the south pole, "runs low," and is a *true barometric sign* of warm weather, not from the effect of the moon upon the earth, however, but from a retrocession of the dia electric currents towards the north pole, leaving the sun's rays free to impart *heat,* softening and mellowing the atmosphere into Italian summer skies.

All changes in atmospheric temperature are caused by the variations of the dia electric currents, as well as all "signs" of storm, wind, calm, heat, cold, aurora borealis, and meteoric phenomena—the abundant shower and the refreshing dew. These electric variations sensibly affect vegetation, augment and diminish the flow of vital fluid, by infusing, under one set of circumstances, a greater amount of electric or negative fluid into all vegetable forms, and under another set of circumstances infusing a greater amount of positive fluid into the same forms, which renders it highly probable that the *health* of animals as well as persons is affected by those who partake of them. Thus we may safely arrive at a solution of the problem, the origin of disease, and, having ascertained the *cause,* may we not reasonably look for a *remedy* in the appliances of electric agents?

Disease may be resolved into two classes, namely, *positive* and *negative.* All fevers being positive, and all colds or chronics being negative, they should be treated accordingly.

"The Moon affects the tides."
When mind meets mind, then comes the test of strength. ,

Now, in contradiction to the established and popular theory that the moon affects the tides, I propose to show that they are the effects of the rotary and pendulum-like movement of the earth itself; as, for instance, when the earth is in a certain position upon its axis, the ocean masses flow back upon uniform currents, causing an ebb tide at a particular point, and during six hours the earth

turns one-fourth upon its axis, causing a flow tide to commence at
the first point, and an ebb tide to commence at a second point, thus
onward around the earth, the tides varying according to time and
the relative position of the planet upon its axis, all of which facts
may be demonstrated by taking observations at different localities
throughout the world, noting the time and duration of tides, the
inclination of the earth, and its position upon its axis.

Wind is a current of dense or *cold* atmosphere propelled by
electricity, always flowing in uniform surface currents from the
poles towards the equator, where it rarifies by the heat of the sun's
rays, ascends, and flows back in an elevated strata to either pole
again.

These elevated strata of heated atmosphere flowing uniformly
from the equator to the poles may reasonably account for open
seas in those localities, or temperate zones developing an advanced state of vegetation.

Cross or counter currents of wind are dense or cold volumes of
atmosphere propelled by electricity, arising from the surface of
large bodies of water, elevated portions of land, mountain sum-
mits, and snow-capped peaks, rushing forward to equalize the temperature of valleys, plains, and equatorial regions, rarified and
expanded by the heat of the sun's rays. This law of equilibrium,
everywhere manifest in nature, demonstrates beyond refutation
that the laws of attraction and repulsion are *the* positive and negative laws governing and developing all organic forms. Nowhere
in art are these laws more beautifully illustrated than in the application of steam as a motive power. Water is the cold or negative
element, and fuel the positive, each containing in prescribed limits
their respective force in concentrated form, and, being placed in
juxtaposition to each other, the fuel is ignited, decomposing its
mass, and generating heat or the positive force, which infuses itself into the watery element, repelling the electricity or negative
force inherent in the water, which seeks to escape from confine-
ment, carrying with it particles of moisture, thus generating what
is popularly called "the motive power of steam." Here the positive repels the negative, manifesting motion while under restraint,
but so soon as set free the equilibrium is restored by each reverting immediately into those concentrated forms or substances for
which they have an affinity.

The same laws hold good in the physical organism of animal
and human forms, the positive or magnetic law of heat having its
seat in the cerebrum, and the negative or animal electric law
having its seat in the cerebellum; the first existing in and operating on the sympathetic nerves, and the second existing in and operating on the muscular nerves, expanding and contracting the
muscles in obedience to the dictates of the will. Thus are all

human actions performed, which are simply the external manifestations of the spiritual Being within.

Having now partially redeemed my promise by barely touching upon great subjects, I submit the foregoing suggestions in brief to an impartial public, not claiming for them absolute perfection, but as approaching nearer the truth than the old theories, and eminently worthy a candid consideration.

Very truly, yours, CITETUS.

WASHINGTON, D. C., *May* 23, 1857.

J. M. PECK, Esq., *Rockspring, Illinois*:

DEAR SIR: By the politeness of a very highly distinguished friend and gentleman, the *Missouri Republican* of the 3d of May, containing a letter from your pen has this moment been handed me for perusal.

An extract from a private letter published by me in the *National Intelligencer* of April 17, 1857, is made the basis of your communication.

I am happy to have it in my power to refer your attempted quotations from my note back to you for *correction*, as I never advanced such ideas as you force me give utterance to, nor does your argument *touch* the new theories suggested in my note, or assign a *cause* for the "local causes" set forth in your dissertation on "*storms.*"

You must have observed ere this, that the note from which you attempted to quote, was published for the purpose of drawing out the communications that followed, and are now to be found in the *National Intelligencer* of May 1st, 11th, and 21st, over the signature of "Citetus."

It affords me pleasure to refer you to those articles, and recommend a careful perusal of them, after which I shall be most happy to receive your opinion of their merits, either private or through the public press. Very truly yours, CITETUS.

(GEORGE B. SIMPSON.)

P. S.—*Messrs. Editors Republican*: GENTLEMEN: Should you decline publishing this note, do me the favor to forward it to Mr. Peck, and oblige, yours, &c., G. B. S.

ULTIMATES.

LIFE.

The great object of life is to learn *how* to *live*.
Death can have no *terrors* if we *live rightly*.

TIME.

What is time? Moments measured by a dial. Are not these moments atomic periods of the great eternity? Are they not periods of *the* eternity in which ADAM *lives?* Where *is* ADAM? Certainly *not here,* but *in* eternity. Is eternity, then, separate and distinct *from* time; or, are these terms synonymous, distinguished *only* by a *state* of *Being?* If this be true, then we should speak of the *condition,* not the *fact,* as *in* time and *in* eternity, for, if *time* signify *eternity,* why, then, whatever term we apply can only refer to the *state* and not the *period* of duration. Thus *we live in eternity,* and have only to change *our condition* to be with ADAM.

BELIEF.

What is *belief?* Simply an *opinion* of something which *may* and *may not* be true.

The *present* is all man ever enjoys.

Free thought and unrestricted research is the province of rational minds.

Childhood's sports, manhood's plays,
Improve our morals, mend our ways.

To be, or *change* and be, for man is and is to be.

VIRTUE.

What is virtue? It is the crucifiction of the animal or worldly appetites, passions, and desires *in* man; for, if these are not to be subdued, cut up by the roots, and entirely eradicated from the human heart by the exercise of *Reason* and *fortitude,* why, then, *there can be no virtue in overcoming;*

This is that precept of APPOLLO: *"Know thyself."*

Love is a divine attribute of God *within* us.

There is no darkness only in the mind of man where ignorance dwells. What a commentary on the Christian *Era?*

Life is the chrysalis state of man; death (so called) the blooming of the spirit.

The good are always happy.

So let me *live* as that my retrospect shall gather no *regrets* from my *memory.*

Memory is the *Record* of our *deeds,* which is the " BOOK " that will be "*opened*" and read—by whom? By him who has a *right* to judge and award judgment—THYSELF.

We can meditate no wrong, do no wrong whose wound is not inflicted on our own memory! Alas, *can* the blood of Calvery efface the evil thought, the evil deed? Trust it not, but *keep the memory free.*

3

DEATH.

What is death? It is simply the *separation* of the *positive* from the *negative*, or the *internal* from the *external* FORM; literally, there *is no death*; nothing *dies, ever!* Simply, composition, *de*composition, and *recomposition*; this is the whole round and *formula* of Nature, therefore *forms* were all that were ever *created. New forms* are incessantly springing into Being, exemplifying the *life-creative* principle inherent in matter, which is the *"life"* and the *"word,"* which *"was* GOD."

HEAT.

All heat is generated by *abrasion. Solar* heat is *evolved* by the *friction* of the sun's rays upon the *atmosphere. Artificial* heat is evolved by the *friction of dissolving* substances; and the passage of currents of *electricity* over dense metals, such as platina wire, &c., &c., even to fusion and dissolution.

COLD.

Heat and *cold* are simply positive and negative electricity. Substances are simply concentrated *forms* of electricity, all of which *forms*, when dissolved, revert to electric *force*, or *first* principles, and are *ever active*, exemplifying the *life* of matter.

PROSPERITY.

Be *just* and *love* Woman, and all other good things will be added unto you.

GEORGE B. SIMPSON.

WASHINGTON, D. C., *June* 20, 1859.

ELECTRIC HEAT AND MOTIVE POWER.

WASHINGTON, *September* 27, 1859.

To the Editors of the National Intelligencer :

GENTLEMEN: On the 20th instant a patent issued to the undersigned for an apparatus for generating *heat* by electricity. This is the first step towards the attainment of a great end, namely, the development of *light, heat, and motive power* by electricity, and its successful application to the uses of man. The generation of light and heat by electricity in diminutive quantities and under peculiar circumstances is not new, but the *mode of controling and applying* it to the ordinary uses of life is new and has been patented.

The ELECTRO HEATER is somewhat costly in its construction, but when once put into practical operation its primary value never diminishes, the wear and tear of the apparatus is merely nominal, and the expense of generating heat sufficient to warm and cook for an ordinary family and house will not exceed *ten dollars per year*. Chimneys, fire-places, coal and wood stoves may all be abandoned; and indeed the Electro Heater may be placed in a parlor in any desired form or in any piece of elegant furniture, and cooking may there be performed with impunity without ashes, dust, or smoke; and for warming purposes it may be similarly situated with like results.

The heating surface may be of any required dimensions, from which surface heat is obtained by passing currents of electricity over a platinum helical electrode. The only labor required to operate the Heater is simply the connecting and disconnecting of the electric current by touching a key like the key of a piano. By connecting the electric current the helical electrode is immediately reduced to a red or a white-red heat, which rarifies and expands the air in contact with it, causing it to ascend, producing thereby a comparative vacuum, into which vacuum the cold air in a room is immediately impelled, which, in its turn, is heated or rarified and ascends, thus creating a current of air sweeping over the surface of the Heater, which will continue, if no air is permitted to escape from the room and no cold to enter, until the mass is in equilibrium, or is of the same temperature as the Heater. Thus it will be perceived that the saving of heat by this process is about as 100 is to 1—that is to say, by the ordinary process of generating heat by the decomposition of wood and coal and the consequent creation of an ascending current of rarified air, 100 parts of the heat thus generated passes up and out at the top of the chimney into the common air, while by the new electrical process *one part* will not thus escape; therefore a great saving of *heat* as well as money in generating it is obtained.

By touching the key and disconnecting the electric current the Heater immediately cools.

Your obedient servant,   GEORGE B. SIMPSON.

[Correspondence of the Decatur Weekly Magnet.]

DECATUR, ILLINOIS, Saturday Morning, *October* 8, 1859.

Mr. George B. Simpson has just taken out a patent for an instrument to supply heat and motive power by electricity. He calls it the "Electro Heater," and claims that the saving by it will be as one hundred to one. The construction of the apparatus will be rather costly, but will render chimneys, fire-pipes, and wood or coal stoves totally unnecessary. It may be placed in any part of a room, *ad libitum*, and can be made as an elegant piece of furniture. The cost of cooking and warming by it, for an ordinary

sized family, he estimates at about ten dollars per annum. There
is no labor about the apparatus, as the heat is let on or stopped
off at pleasure, by merely touching a key like the key of a piano.

PROPOSALS FOR THE NEW ATLANTIC CABLE.—*New York, August* 19, 1859.—
The Atlantic Telegraph Company have issued an invitation to inventors, patentees,
and manufacturers of submarine cables, to come forward as soon as possible with
specimens and plans of cables suitable for ocean service, to be submitted to the
Company for examination, testing, and experiment.

The invitation extends to all persons engaged in business, in whatever country
residing; the object being to get the very best cable that can be produced. All
communications to be addressed to the Secretary of the Company, George Saward,
22 Old Broad Street, London.

WASHINGTON, D. C., *September* 10, 1859.

GEORGE SAWARD, Esq.,

22 *Old Broad Street, London, England:*

SIR: Mind, matter, and Motion, are the elementary principles
of all conceivable effects. Intelligence supreme, Matter divisible
and indestructible, Motion infinite in duration and infinite in application.

These three primary essences constitute the God-head, of which
the Father, Son, and Holy Ghost are typical. They are in substance One, performing three distinct offices in the order named ;
Intelligence to conceive and direct, Matter to form and transform,
and Motion to transfer the will and the particle in obedience to
the dictates of the infinite and rightly exalted Supreme Reason.
This trinity of essences, substances, forces, exist in and constitute
every part and particle of the whole material universe. They are
of, in, and unto the great original first cause. They are God, and
all effects are but the expression of His will.

All forms, whether gross or refined, animate or inanimate, are
first conceived, then organized by the concentration of particles
having an affinity of soceal qualities, being transferred by the
power of motion. The existence of this trinity of essences and
forces may be demonstrated by the analysis of any conceivable
material form.

In the human kingdom they may be designated by the terms
Mind, Matter, and Magnetism; in the animal kingdom they may
be designated by the terms Instinct, Matter, and Animal Electricity; in the vegetable kingdom they are Solid, Fluid, and Electric ; in the inorganic substances they are Solid, Liquid, and Aireform ; the vital forces are everywhere the same, being modified in
all cases to conform to the gross or refined unfolded and unfolding
forms. From these deductions we find that Electricity is probably
the third elementary principle of the God-head, that its attributes
are Deatic, and that it permeates all substances ; as such we must

consider it if we would arrive at a satisfactory solution of the problem, or a rational understanding of its effects.

Electricity, then, may be regarded as one of the elementary principles of primary substances, and is, perhaps, too sublimated to be perceived by the human mind ; its effects, however, may be observed and considered. There is, there can be no effect in Nature not dependant on and immediately traceable to electricity ; it is the motive power of all organic and inorganic as well as all animate and inanimate forms; it holds the planets in their spheres, warms the earth's atmosphere by friction upon its particles, is the subtle fluid existing in the human brain, and moves the strong volume of a muscle ; it is, in a word, all that is possible for the human mind to *know*, far transcending the sublimest thought, the most vivid imagination, the loftiest conception.

It is too universal to be easily understood—its application to the uses and comforts of man is the subject which challenges our investigation at the present time. How shall it be concentrated? How controled? How applied? These are questions requiring practical answers, and I venture with becoming modesty to offer such suggestions as have occurred to my mind.

For more than twenty years I have been a student and a close observer of the phenomena of Nature. I was seven years endeavoring to insulate the telegraph wire, and, finally, on the 22d day of November, 1847, I discovered a process of insulation ; it was as follows : The wire was first insulated with India rubber or gutta percha, then covered with glass beads closely socketed and jointed together, over which was drawn an insoluble India rubber hose, which was fastened to the beads by being pressed into grooves by twining iron bands or hempen cords around them at convenient distances from each other, thus making a submarine telegraph cable at once flexible and convenient, and perfect in all its practical tests and applications. I have since abandoned the external hose and glass beads, retaining only the gutta percha as an insulator, and for which an application asking letters patent of the United States is still pending in our Patent Office. I hereby announce to the world my claim to this invention, and warn all telegraph companies and others not to use it under penalty of the law. (This, of course, applies to America.) In my opinion, a single wire properly insulated with gutta percha will be more certain of success than a combination of wires in laying a cable across the Atlantic ocean—the feasibility of which was suggested by me as early as 1847.

In connection with this subject, I may suggest that I think it highly probable that a gutta percha tube one and a half inch in diameter and one half or three quarter inch bore, filled with water, will prove the cheapest and most effective submarine telegraph cable. Water is quite as good a conductor of electricity as metal, and it is possible that a tube thus filled with fresh water will sink in the ocean salt water to a depth only of its own specific density. This will avoid the possibility of a *break* in the water or electric current, (as is supposed by some to be the case with the wire cable recently laid,) and form, by connecting links, a network of ocean telegraph which will unite every portion of the habitable globe, and concentrate, in accordance with my suggestion of 1847, the intelligence of the world in one common centre—at a given point.

I may venture another suggestion, which, if acted on, may prove of service to mankind. An air tube, sunk in the ocean like the water tube above named, may serve as a speaking-trumpet, through which oral messages may be communicated with equal facility and greater certainty than the electric current.

I have other inventions in electricity of great value and importance to the world, but it might be considered out of place to enumerate them here.

Hoping the suggestions I have made may be of interest to you, and wishing you entire success in the great enterprise of laying the Atlantic cable, and begging you to accept my kind regards,

I remain, sir, very respectfully, your obedient servant,

GEORGE B. SIMPSON.

THE MAMMOTH BALLOON.

To the Editors of the National Intelligencer:

GENTLEMEN: In 1856 I published my views on aerial currents prevailing on the west coast of America and the Pacific ocean, and in May, 1857, I published in your valuable journal my views on uniform and counter wind currents in all parts of the world, and showed, I think, that they are all impelled by the motive power of electricity. However this may be, it is not now the point under consideration, but *the* current which is to waft the great balloon from the shores of America to the shores of England.

It is highly probable that all the great uniform wind currents of the world are directed in their course by the great ocean currents which flow beneath them. If this be true, then, if Professor Lowe will transfer his starting point from New York city to the Island of Cuba, and ascend in the aerial current indicated by the Gulf Stream, he may pass the eastern coast of the northern half of this continent and reach England within the time indicated in his programme. Again, if he ascend at New York city in a current flowing from west to east, he *may* reach the great ocean current indicated by the Gulf Stream, and thus achieve the object of his experiment. Currents counter to the great uniform wind currents in all parts of the world are alike subject to the electrical conditions of the atmosphere.

Your obedient servant,   GEORGE B. SIMPSON.

WASHINGTON, D. C., *November* 15, 1859.

———

REAPPEARANCE OF THE RINGS OF SATURN.—On Tuesday, (to-day,) August 12, the Rings of Saturn will again be seen, having been wholly invisible, except through the most powerful telescopes, nearly three months. In the course of the last eight months these rings have twice disappeared, the first time from November 23 to January 31, in consequence of their edge being turned towards the earth, and the second time, or since May 17, their unilluminated side. Through powerful telescopes the ring at the first disappearance could, however, be seen, as a straight line, and at the second the ansae or extremities were still visible.

During those interesting periods the appearance of Saturn and its rings has been carefully watched by astronomers, and in a communication to the London Astronomical Society, at its last meeting, that excellent observer, Rev. W. R. Dawes, says: "Nothing, I imagine, can more fully prove the *almost inconceivable thinness of the rings* than the absence of all perceptible shadow. Had it even the *least* thickness which has ever been ascribed to it, (*forty* miles by Professor Bond, Director of Harvard College Observatory, Cambridge, United States,) it would be sufficient to produce a total eclipse of the sun on Saturn's equator, as it would subtend an angle more than double that subtended by the disk of the sun as seen from Saturn.

For an explanation of the rings of Saturn, I respectfully beg leave to refer the reader to my letter addressed to Samuel L. Morton, Esq., dated Cincinnati, Ohio, May 10, 1851, and published for the first time in this series.

If electrical, as I affirm, their apparent disappearance would simply indicate a *change of position*, in which position they, the electric rings, so called, are incapable of refracting light.

In illustration of this fact, I might instance the rain-bow; which, when we are in a certain position, appears bright and beautiful, and when we are in a different position does not appear at all.

· So with the aurora borealis ; under cirtain conditions of the atmosphere this auroral light appears bright and beautiful, and under different conditions of the atmosphere the auroral light does not appear at all.

So with the rings of Saturn : when in a proper *position* they become visible to us, not from the tangibility of their substance, but from their ability electrically to refract light.

The rings are, therefore, sufficiently tangible to appear luminous to our sense of sight, but not to our sense of touch, unless, indeed, we were to pass through them, in which event we would congeal, as they exemplify the negative organic law inherent in all matter, which is *cold*, or electricity.

GEORGE B. SIMPSON.

WASHINGTON, D. C., *September*, 1862.

A "Disappearance."—The discovery of the disappearance of one or two nebulæ in the heavens has excited the liveliest interest among astronomers. So unlooked-for a phenomenon fairly startles the hardest understanding. Objects hitherto regarded as firm, enduring, and fixed as the pillars of the universe, have been found as unstable as an autumnal meteor. What great revolution in astronomy is about to be made no one can conjecture. The awful mystery only heightens on reflection; and vague, shadowy forebodings of the "rottenness of the pillared firmament" crowd upon the imagination.—*Boston Courier.*

If, as is alleged in this paragraph, certain nebulæ have disappeared from the heavens, it is not improbable that they may be obscured by the intervention of opaque bodies between us and them and not discernable by us, and will, therefore, reappear again when those opaque bodies shall have passed.

Have no fears of the "rottenness of the pillared firmament," as matter is indestructible, and *change of form* the law, immutable as God, and that anything that *is* cannot be destroyed, and therefore must continue to be "regarded as firm, enduring, and fixed as the pillars of the universe."

God and Nature is, and we shall continue to be, though *changed* it may be.

Read these brief pages and be cheered with the assurance that Nature is divine, truth is immortal, and that *nothing but Error can perish.*

The existence of *fear* is the strongest evidence of *error.*

Where *Truth* is there is *hope*, light, life, and immortality.

And when we *know* that matter is indestructible, and that *forms* only change, we also *know* that our interior *Being* cannot be annihilated, but that it *must* exist, if not in this state certainly in a *better one*, as no form can *descend below* its own development, but must *ascend* in the scale and order of creation.

Therefore there can be no *fear* for the perpetuity of the universe "*so long as Reason is left free to combat error.*"

GEORGE B. SIMPSON.

WASHINGTON, D. C., *September*, 1862.

——o——

High o'er the crest of infant years mayest thou soar, O Man; ascend the height of hoary ages, and on the dial of eternal time, write, Alpha!

GEORGE B. SIMPSON.

www.ingramcontent.com/pod-product-compliance
Lightning Source LLC
Chambersburg PA
CBHW031759090426
42739CB00008B/1077